Culture Code Breaker
When Oppression Wears Lipstick and Heels

Leslie Baker

Copyright © 2025 B3-Cubed, LLC

All rights reserved. No part of this book may be reproduced in any manner without the express written consent of the author, except in the case of brief excerpts in critical reviews or articles. All inquiries should be addressed to: B3cubedllc@gmail.com.

Paperback ISBN: 979-8-218-72337-8

DEDICATION

To Mike E - boss, mentor, and lifelong friend. You know the truths in these pages, and you're wise enough to know no man should ever say them aloud.

CONTENTS

Acknowledgments	i
When Sabotage Wears Heels	9
Unspoken Battles	11
The "B" Word	15
High Heels, Low Blows	23
Who Built The Culture	31
Perception Is Reality	39
Don't Weaponize Your Insecurities	45
Mistakes Will Be Magnified	51
A+ Students Don't Mean A+ Professionals	55
No One's Tossing A Life Raft	59
The Invisible Wall	65
Your Superpower	69
Neon Cellphone	75
Clothes Talk	79
You Can't Unpost Your Reputation	83
Love and Paychecks Don't Mix	89
This Is Not His Fight	95
The Breakroom Is Not a Therapy Room	99
Negativity Train	105
Emotional Labor 101	113
Boss ≠ Friend	119
Professional Etiquette	123
Lost Skills That Still Matter	127
The Ending is the Beginning	131
Culture Code Recap	135

ACKNOWLEDGMENTS

To the women who underestimated me, doubted me, or tried to silence me, you became the reason I wrote louder. To the women who stood beside me, you became the reason I finished.

WHEN SABOTAGE WEARS HEELS

The Conversation that Sparked it All

This book started with a conversation at a kitchen table between me, a close friend, and her daughter - a freshly minted Gen Z graduate ready to blow up every broken system in her path. She had a plan: no shaving, neon hair, and full rebellion against "the man." I loved her fire - I really did. But when she declared, without hesitation, that all the dysfunction in the workplace was because of men, I had to gently hit pause.

"What if the biggest obstacle to women… isn't men?" I asked.

She blinked. I waited. And that uncomfortable question cracked something open. That conversation turned into a mission and that mission became this book. This is the book I wish someone had handed me on day one, not to scare me, but to prepare me.

In these pages, I'll show you the patterns women rarely speak about, why they exist, and most importantly, how you can protect yourself and rise above them.

What They Said vs. What I Saw

My friend's daughter's energy reminded me of so many new hires I've seen walk through corporate doors: ambitious, idealistic, and unprepared for the politics they were about to walk into. I've spent over twenty years in the trenches of Human Resources, and I've seen the same messages recycled repeatedly - posters promoting sisterhood, seminars declaring "empowered women empower women," and corporate trainings filled with talk of collaboration, empathy, and inclusion among women. But every time I've come across one of these messages, I can't help but think:

"Why won't anyone just say what's really happening? Why won't anyone be real?"

I'm here to let you know a secret that no one is telling you: the workplace can be brutal, and sometimes, the harshest critics aren't men, they're other women. We know it. We've seen it. Some of us have even lived it. So why has no one been willing to say the problem aloud?

Here's the good news: once you see the patterns clearly, you don't have to internalize them, you can prepare for them, respond differently, and even break the cycle.

That's why I authored this book. *Culture Code Breaker: When Oppression Wears Lipstick and Heels* is about what really happens behind office doors. It shows the subtle ways women undermine each other, such as the silent power plays, and the passive-aggressive comments disguised as "just being honest."

The chapters that follow reveal what school didn't teach you, but what's essential for navigating today's workplace. *Culture Code Breaker* will instruct you on how to recognize sabotage, understand generational dynamics, spot red flags, and protect your energy, without shrinking your ambition. *Culture Code Breaker* is not another feel-good book filled with pretty quotes and generic advice. It's direct, unapologetic, and designed to equip, not entertain. It's a practical field manual that finally tells the truth about what happens between women at work. I've seen bright women shrink to fit in, new hires crushed by office politics by lunch, and people-pleasers burn out chasing praise they'll never get.

Not only will this book tell you what to expect, it will equip you with real tools to handle it. You'll find thought-provoking worksheets at the end of key chapters to help you reflect, prepare, and figure out how you want to show up in this space, especially when you cross paths with difficult women in the future. You can skip the worksheets and still get the message. However, I encourage you to do the work now, so your future self walks in with more confidence, precision, and resilience than you ever thought possible. You'll learn how to spot subtle sabotage, how to redirect it without shrinking, and how to create micro-moments of culture change—even if you're the youngest in the room.

Consider This Your Head Start

If your early experience with women at work has been all high-fives and supportive group chats, hold onto that, it's rare. But for many, the reality will include being talked over, dismissed, or quietly undermined… sometimes by the very people who preach teamwork and empowerment.

Don't wait for workplace culture to fix itself, be the woman who sets a new standard. You weren't made just to survive your career, but to lead, grow, and pave the way for those who come next. This book is here to give you that head start. The stilettos might be sharp, but your awareness will be sharper, because you took the time to prepare, learn, and invest in yourself.

If there's one truth, I want you to carry from this book is: awareness is your power. See the patterns for what they are, and you'll shape your career on your terms, not theirs

Now, let's get to work.

UNSPOKEN BATTLES

A Light in the Dark.
School prepared you for presentations, not power plays. Sure, you learned how to write essays, analyze case studies, and build a killer PowerPoint, but nobody warned you about the cold stares across the conference table, the email exclusions, or the subtle eye rolls by someone you thought was on your side. *Culture Code Breaker* isn't a textbook; it's a mirror, a megaphone, and a flashlight. After reading this book, you'll see yourself, hear yourself and learn to light a path for others.

Workplace culture isn't crafted by policies; it's shaped by whispers, side glances and who gets invited to happy hour. It's formed in how you respond to someone else's success, how you speak about your colleagues behind closed doors, and what you are willing to tolerate in silence.

The truth is, much of this quiet culture-shaping doesn't come from men in corner offices, it comes from women, often unintentionally passing down patterns they once endured themselves.

HR Story Time
Let me take you back to my first job. I showed up beaming, wearing a skirt that still had the price tag on it, and enough enthusiasm to power a startup. By day three, however, a senior woman on the team pulled me aside and said, "Tone it down. The women here don't like show-offs."

Show-off? I hadn't even had my first client meeting yet, but my energy, my outfit, and the sparkle in my eyes were already "too much." I learned quickly that excellence can make people uncomfortable.

Fast-forward twenty years, and guess what? I'm still "accidentally" getting left off email threads, dismissed in meetings, and watching my ideas get recycled by someone else with less insight and way more applause. Turns out experience doesn't make you immune to office nonsense. And a lot of that resistance? Still coming from other women. Only now, we've dressed it up: it's not sabotage, it's "constructive feedback;"

or it's not jealousy, it's "concern about team dynamics;" and my personal favorite, it's not exclusion, it's "just a misunderstanding."

What I eventually realized is that these weren't random one-offs—they were part of a larger pattern women quietly repeat. And once you see the pattern, you stop doubting yourself and start making a difference.

Workplace Oppression in Lipstick.

You may not control how others treat you, but you do control how you respond and what you carry forward. The cycle of silence, competition, and coldness can end with you. And while burnout may have been baked into the culture long before you got there, it doesn't have to continue your watch. You didn't create the dysfunction, but you can be the one who refuses to keep it alive.

If you've made mistakes before—like staying quiet or protecting yourself at someone else's expense—you're not alone. Growth begins when we name it, own it, and commit to behaving differently.

What a Healed Culture Looks Like:

Meet Zoe. She was 28, new to management, and overseeing a team where gossip used to thrive. In her first meeting, she set a team norm: no one talks about co-workers unless they're in the room. It was awkward, but it worked. Within weeks, her team started speaking up, solving problems together, and trusting each other. One boundary shifted the entire dynamic.

I once coached a department where trust had been fractured for years. After six months of honesty forums, establishing team norms, and leadership modeling transparency, women started giving credit freely, looping each other in proactively, and even holding 'Donut Fridays' to spotlight peer wins. It wasn't perfect, but it was progress.

Notice how these changes directly counter the very patterns we talked about: exclusion replaced with inclusion, criticism replaced with recognition.
You get to stop the cycle.

Surviving in the workplace isn't about climbing the ladder, it's about understanding the obstacles in your way. Getting there is only part of the battle. What really matters is whether you make the path smoother or harder for the women coming behind you, because if the culture, bias, or barriers you will fight to overcome stay the same, was your struggle to succeed worth it?

So, what does it really mean to be that someone for the next woman in line? It starts with telling the truth about what "women oppressing women" sometimes looks like in real life.

The Other Side of "Women Supporting Women"

Undermining among women in the workplace often hides behind polished

professionalism. It's not always loud or obvious, but it's effective. These behaviors quietly erode trust, credibility, and collaboration. The examples below show just how subtle—and damaging—undermining can be:
- A co-worker who consistently "forgets" to include you on key emails while keeping others in the loop.
- A manager who presents your ideas as their own in leadership meetings, then reminds you, *"We're all one team."*
- Public praise followed by private criticism—subtle enough to avoid formal complaints but strong enough to shake your confidence.
- Corrections made during meetings—not to clarify, but to diminish—without ever offering constructive feedback one-on-one.

If these examples feel surprising, that's because no one warns you about them before you step into the workplace. That's where awareness becomes your edge: you can't strategize against what you can't see. The first step in protecting yourself isn't retaliation, it's recognition.

It's not just you.

This behavior isn't random, it's patterned. It's part of a harmful legacy passed down in workplaces where scarcity ruled and women had to compete for scraps. And now? It's your job to recognize it, name it, and choose not to replicate it. Seeing it clearly is the first step to stopping it, for yourself, and for the next woman coming up behind you.

Understanding the "Why" Doesn't Excuse the Behavior, but It Can Help You Rise Above It

It's tempting to take workplace oppression personally, especially when it's coming from other women. But often, their actions have less to do with *you* and more to do with the wounds, fears, and survival strategies they've carried into the workplace. Women who undermine other women often:

- **Were once undermined themselves and internalized it as a rite of passage**. They endured criticism, exclusion, and silent treatment, and now believe that "if I survived it, so should you."
- **Feel threatened by someone who's younger, more educated, more confident, or simply different**. Your presence challenges their sense of relevance or security, especially in environments where women have been pitted against each other.
- **Think that tough love equals leadership.** They confuse criticism with coaching and believe withholding support makes you stronger. They were taught that kindness is weakness and now pass that lesson down like its wisdom.

- **Still play by outdated rules from a time when success was scarce, and women had to work twice as hard just to be seen.** Those rules of keeping their guard up, protecting their turf, and not trusting anyone may have served them once, but they've become a source of harm now.

HR Story: When Tough Love Turns Toxic

In a memorable coaching session, a high-potential employee opened up about the silent tension between her and her direct manager. She was smart, driven, and eager to grow, but she kept hitting a wall. Her manager, a long-tenured female leader in the department, rarely gave her feedback, guidance, or direction. No goals, no check-ins and no recognition, just silence and vague expectations.

When the employee finally worked up the courage to ask for clarity, the response was short and sharp:

"You need to figure it out on your own. That's what I had to do."

That manager thought she was building resilience; that letting her direct report "struggle through it" would somehow shape her into a stronger, more independent employee. But what she was really building was resentment. The employee didn't feel empowered, she felt abandoned and set up; like the rules were being kept from her on purpose.

Here's the kicker: this employee didn't *lack* initiative. She had already taken ownership, problem-solved, and sought mentorship elsewhere. What that manager did not realize is this: you don't build strong women by withholding support and calling it leadership. You build strong women by being the person you once needed and choosing to lead differently.

If you've ever been on the receiving end of this kind of 'tough love,' know this: it says more about their insecurity than your ability.

Hurt Women Hurt Women.

You don't have to internalize the mistreatment, and you *don't* have to repeat it. When you understand *why* it happens, you can stop wondering, *"what's wrong with me"*? Instead of playing the victim, you can shift to strategist and choose to work differently without playing small, getting bitter, or becoming the next woman who repeats the cycle. Awareness is step one. Step two is learning how to protect your confidence and achieve success, even when sabotage shows up.

THE "B" WORD

I once overheard two directors whispering about a senior female leader: *"She's great,"* one said. *"But man, she's a total bitch when she wants something."*

Translation: assertive, focused, direct , and too powerful for their comfort. Language shapes perception, and perception shapes opportunity. If we don't call out how terms like the "B" word are used to silence women, we reinforce the same power dynamics that keep us small.

The "B" word is one of the most loaded, weaponized words used against women. It's a verbal grenade designed to explode credibility, confidence, and composure in one syllable. It doesn't matter whether you're climbing the corporate ladder, leading a project, or simply holding a boundary, the moment you stop making yourself small to keep others comfortable, the label might find its way to you. And you'll likely hear it whispered in the hallways, muttered under breaths, or flat-out shouted, whether behind your back or, if you're unlucky, to your face.

Where Did the Word Come From?

To understand the weight this word carries, we need to go back.

The "B" word first appeared in Old English as *bicce* around the 1400s and it simply meant a female dog. It wasn't derogatory; it was descriptive. But as early as the 15th and 16th centuries, society began attaching moral judgment to female behavior, especially around sexuality and obedience. By the 18th century, the "B" word was a direct insult to women, paired with accusations of promiscuity or disobedience.

By the 19th century, the term solidified as a gendered insult for women who didn't conform to the passive, delicate, domestic ideal. A woman who spoke her mind, pursued independence, or displayed ambition outside the home was labeled unnatural — and the "B" word became the go-to leash to keep her in place.

The 20th century, especially the feminist waves of the 1920s and 1970s, intensified this backlash. Women in public roles were no longer just "wrong," they were "bitches." Media followed suit, portraying ambitious women as villains, cementing the word as shorthand for "a woman who refuses to obey."

What this history reveals are striking: every time women advanced socially or politically, the language against them sharpened. The "B" word became more than a slur. It became a tool to control, categorize, and punish.

And it's still working. Even today, the word carries centuries of cultural baggage.

> 💬 *"When a man gives his opinion, he's a man. When a woman gives hers, she's a "B.""* - Bette Davis

What the "B" Word Really Means

Here's the truth: the "B" word has nothing to do with your behavior and everything to do with someone else's discomfort. It's shorthand for saying:

- "You're not making it easy for me."
- "You're not doing what I want."
- "You're taking up space I didn't expect you to take."

And it's almost always said by someone who feels threatened, not genuinely offended.

> 💬 *"I'm tough, I'm ambitious, and I know exactly what I want. If that makes me a "B," okay."* - Madonna

So, the next time you hear it, aimed at you or another woman, pause and decode what's really being said. Most of the time, it has more to do with them than it ever will with you.

A Word with Teeth

Here's where it gets more damaging: Men didn't just use the term. Women started using it against each other, too. If one woman pushed too hard, dressed too confidently, or climbed too fast, she risked being branded with the word by her peers.

It became a way to regulate women's behavior, to keep each other "in line". That's how the "B" word transformed from a label to a weapon: a way to punish power, not unruly behavior.

Let's stop pretending the "B" word is just a word. It's a warning shot. When certain words are used to diminish women's power, success, and voice, we need to call them out and take back the narrative.

Does reclaiming the word work? Maybe. Some women wear it proudly, flipping the insult into a badge of strength. Others reject it outright, refusing to let it define or describe them.

There's no one right way. But there is one truth: you are not the problem just because you refuse to make yourself smaller.

You Won't Hear the Word, But You'll Know It's There

In most workplaces, no one will call you the "B" word outright. Corporate culture has polished its vocabulary. Today, coded words like *difficult, abrasive, intimidating,* or *not a team player* are the new daggers.

But don't be fooled. Behind closed doors, inside chats and group texts, the word is still there, and often it's coming from another woman.

That's the gut punch. While you're working hard to prove yourself, someone else may quietly slap the label on you for the very traits that make you effective. And instead of confronting you directly, they let the word do the work: undermining your influence, isolating you, or quietly slowing your progress.

How to Defuse the Label

You can't always stop the word from surfacing, but you *can* strip it of its power. Here's how:

- **Decode it.** When you hear "abrasive" or "too direct," ask yourself: *Is this about my competence, or their comfort?*
- **Document it.** If the coded language shows up in reviews or promotion conversations, keep a record. It's not just a word; it's a pattern worth tracking.
- **Redirect it.** Refuse to shrink. Instead, let your results and professionalism speak louder than the label.

The Mic Drop

The "B" word is not a reflection of who you are. It's a mirror showing someone else's discomfort with your strength. You can't always stop the label from surfacing, but you can redefine what it means. The moment you realize that the "B" word is code for "a woman who refuses to shrink," you win. Awareness turns insult into insight and that's your edge.

BEFORE THE WORKPLACE REWRITES YOU
Capture Your Career Mindset Before It Gets Reframed by Reality

Before we dive into office culture truths, red flags, workplace strategies, and how not to lose your identity somewhere between the microwave and the Monday staff meeting, I need you to pause.

Seriously. Pause.

Because before you learn how to read a workplace culture, you've got to be clear on what you expect it to be. What do you believe about work? About leadership? About how women treat each other on the job?

If you don't start by naming your expectations, the workplace will do it for you. And let's be honest: it won't always be pretty.

The Future Culture Worksheet

Before you can recognize culture's games, you need to recognize your own baseline. That's what this exercise captures. Think of the *Future Culture Worksheet* as a time capsule, or a career selfie. Not the filtered kind. The real, unedited snapshot of what you currently think working life will be like, shaped by things like:

- TikTok snippets about quitting corporate life to sell candles on Etsy.
- Advice from mentors who swear "just work hard and everything will fall into place."
- Sitcom bosses who are somehow both charming and morally bankrupt.

Wherever your impressions come from, now's the time to name them, capture them, and own them.

Why This Actually Matters

This isn't busy work. It's baseline brilliance. Here's why it's worth ten minutes of your time:

1. **It becomes your personal growth tracker.**
   → The difference between what you expect now and what you'll experience later is your growth story. That's how a career builds over time.
2. **It helps you name expectations, before they blindside you.**
   → If you don't name them, someone else will. Usually someone in a corner office with zero emotional intelligence.
3. **It puts you back in control.**
   → Self-awareness is your power move. You can't rewrite harmful culture if you don't know what story you started with.

One Rule: No Co-Authors

Start this reflection without anyone else's voice in the room. Don't phone a friend, post it in a group chat, or ask a parent or professor who once called you "promising." The world will try to shape your perspective soon enough — don't start off by borrowing someone else's. The most powerful script you'll ever write is the one that starts with your own words.

Your First Work Assignment

Fill out the worksheet, then tuck it away and set a calendar reminder for one year from today. When you open it again, don't cringe, celebrate. That gap between who you were and who you've become? That's growth. It's proof you showed up, stayed present, and did the work.

This worksheet isn't a burden. It's a gift. Your first act of self-leadership. A bold declaration that says:

"I take myself, my future, and my career seriously, even if no one else does yet."

Next year, you'll notice the little shifts: how you define leadership, how you handle conflict, how you've learned to read a room. That's your growth story.

So, pause. Give yourself ten real, no-filter minutes. Then, come back ready.
Because the workplace may try to shape you, but you're already stepping in with your heels on and your eyes wide open.

Future Culture Worksheet

Capture Your Career Mindset Before Reality Reframes It

Take ten quiet minutes to complete this worksheet. There's no right or wrong answer, just your honest baseline. Be real and unfiltered. When you're done, don't peek again until your calendar reminder hits in 12 months.

1. 60-Second Pulse Check (circle 1–5)

1 = strongly disagree · 5 = strongly agree

1. I feel clear about what a healthy culture looks like.	1 2 3 4 5
2. I can spot early red flags in team dynamics.	1 2 3 4 5
3. I know how I'll respond if I'm subtly undermined.	1 2 3 4 5
4. I have at least two people I can go to for candid advice.	1 2 3 4 5
5. I'm confident I can succeed without shrinking myself.	1 2 3 4 5

2. Your Expectations (open reflections)

What do you believe workplace culture should feel like?

What three words describe your ideal workplace?

What behaviors do you expect from a good boss/leader?

How do you think your gender, race, background, or personality may shape your experience?

What worries you most about entering (or being in) the workforce?

What excites you most?

What has most shaped your expectations (school, family, social media, TV, mentors, something else)?

When you picture yourself succeeding at work, what does that look like?

3. Non-Negotiables vs. Flexibles

My 3 non-negotiables for a healthy culture are:

My 3 flexibles (nice to have, not deal-breakers):

4. Red Flags & Boundaries

Top 3 red flags I'll watch for:

My boundary statements (how I'll respond without shrinking):

5. Support Map

Two people I can go to for perspective or coaching:

6. Success Markers (define your "wins")

In 12 months, I'll know I'm on track if…

Set Your Reminder

Today's date: _____

Set a calendar alert for 12 months from today. When it hits, return here and ask:
- What changed? What didn't?
- How did my pulse-check ratings move? Why?
- Which boundaries did I hold? Which do I need to strengthen?

HIGH HEELS, LOW BLOWS

What No One Warns You About

You're ready to crush your first job, armed with a degree, a planner, and a solid work ethic. You expect challenges, sure, but mostly from learning systems, meeting deadlines, and figuring out where they hide the good pens. What you don't expect? That the most confusing, complicated, and sometimes cutthroat part of work... is other women.

You're promised a positive culture, mentorship, open doors, and career development. Instead? Be prepared for cryptic messages, high school lunch table energy, and a whole lot of smiling through confusion while trying not to sink.

Welcome to corporate America!

This doesn't mean every woman you meet will be an obstacle — far from it. But ignoring the reality that some will is the fastest way to be blindsided.

Women in the Workplace: Let's Talk About the Real Issue

If you're a woman - especially a young one - here's what no one says during orientation: sometimes, the hardest part of your job will be other women. You may expect sisterhood, support, and hope for collaboration, connection, and "empowered women empowering women." But often what you'll get:

- Smiles to your face but backstabbing behind closed doors.
- "Feedback" that's really gatekeeping.
- Camaraderie masking as competition.
- Feigned ignorance intended to purposely withhold information.

It's one of the most frustrating-and least discussed-realities of workplace culture. We're not going to ignore it. We're going to name it, unpack it, and give you a plan to break the cycle, without finger-pointing, but with full honesty.

Why It Feels Like Middle School With a 401(k)

Some days, the workplace won't feel like the professional, polished space you imagined. It'll feel like one giant adult playground, except now, the mean girls wear suits, lead meetings, and know how to phrase their insults in perfectly HR-compliant language.

The same clique dynamics you experienced when you were in your eighth-grade homeroom didn't disappear. They just dressed up in corporate jargon and hid behind performance reviews. Instead of "You can't sit with us," you'll hear, "Oh, we had a quick pre-meeting; you must've missed the invite." That juvenile mentality will continue because you'll be judged for things that have nothing to do with your job, like:

- The tone of your voice.
- The clothes you wear.
- The confidence you carry.
- The success you're bold enough to earn.

Seeing it doesn't make it sting less, but it does mean you can prepare instead of personalizing it.

Why Won't They Like You?

Sometimes it won't matter what you do:

- Speak up in meetings? You're "too aggressive."
- Stay quiet? You're "too passive."
- Work late? You're "trying too hard."
- Leave on time? You're "not committed enough."
- Dress up? You're "showing off."
- Dress down? You're "not professional."
- Act confident? You're "cocky."
- Show humility? You "lack presence."

It's a no-win game. And that's the point - if you chase approval, you'll never catch it. Recognizing these contradictions is the first step; next, we'll look at the culture that shaped them.

The Most Painful Part? It's Not Always Intentional.

Not every woman wakes up thinking, "Today I will destroy another woman's confidence." But when we've been socialized to see each other as competition, it happens subconsciously. It shows up in:

- Withholding praise.
- Doubting other's competence.
- Shutting down ideas without discussion.
- Rolling eyes instead of giving feedback.

That's what we must unlearn. The good news? I've watched teams rewrite their norms, where praise is public, feedback is honest, and support is a baseline. Sometimes it's not malicious, it's muscle memory. Once in a meeting I attended, a senior manager took a step back during a heated team meeting and asked a younger employee, "What do you think we should do?" That simple question shifted the tone in the room. Later, the young woman said it was the first time she felt seen as a contributor.

That's why awareness matters, if you catch yourself doing it you can stop the cycle before it spreads.

Signs of Mean Girl Behavior

Adult mean girls don't often throw punches; they disguise them wrapped in smiles and sprinkled with fake support. They've learned how to mask their aggression with just enough polish to avoid being called out. But don't be fooled. If you're not paying attention, their behavior can leave you blindsided, disappointed, and questioning your own judgment.

Below are a few real-life examples of how sabotage often hides behind a friendly face:

The Smile Behind the Sabotage

I've always believed in dressing well for work. It gives me confidence, and I enjoy expressing my personality, especially through bold shoes. One co-worker, who didn't care much for fashion, began complimenting my shoes. At first, it seemed genuine. But over time, those compliments shifted into little digs. She'd make sure to comment in front of others: *"Oh wow, you toned it down today. No bright heels?"* or *"We were all waiting to see what wild shoes you'd show up in this time."* What seemed like kindness at first became a way of questioning my professionalism.

That's the tricky part about this kind of behavior: it doesn't always come at you directly. Sometimes it compliments with a sting. Other times, it's "help" that feels more like public correction. I once watched a colleague repeatedly jump in to rewrite a junior employee's emails and tweak her PowerPoint slides, always in front of others, never in private. On the surface, it looked like mentorship. In reality, it was a way to remind everyone in the room who held the upper hand.

Lesson: Whether it's an excessive compliment or a performative correction, the strategy is the same: masking sabotage as support. Once you recognize it for what it is, you can redirect the focus back to where it belongs: your work.

Supportive Saboteur

At a former company, we had a strong partnership with a major university, bringing in interns for on-the-job training. One finance intern stood out: sharp, driven, and highly regarded. There were even early talks about hiring her full-time after graduation.

She was assigned to assist a senior employee on a federal compliance project. The deadline was serious and missing it meant major penalties. The senior employee played the role of mentor perfectly: warm, friendly, and encouraging. But beneath the surface? Sabotage.

The intern was left scrambling, unsure of the exact steps to complete the task. She spent days at work that should have taken hours. Eventually, she submitted the report, late and inaccurate. Only afterward did we learn that the senior employee had deliberately withheld a binder that outlined the process in detail: which systems to use, what reports to run, and exactly how to compile the data. When asked why she didn't share it, the senior employee shrugged and said, "I forgot I had it." That binder? It was stored in the cabinet above her desk, right next to her daily snack stash.

The intern didn't get the job. The senior employee had to redo the report. And our company's reputation suffered.

Lesson: When someone "forgets" to give you the information you need to succeed, take note. Forgetfulness can be a convenient excuse when someone sees you as competition. True mentors clear paths, not clutter them.

The examples shared should give you a clear picture that some women will smile to your face while quietly working against you behind the scenes. I've seen countless versions of the above behavior over the years; but I've also seen brave women stop the cycle—creating microcultures of trust, transparency, and true collaboration.

Mean girl behavior doesn't disappear after high school, it just matures. It becomes quieter, more strategic, and far more polished. The goal isn't to make you paranoid, it's to make you prepared. Recognize the patterns early - not to fight back - but to protect your progress, your peace, and your confidence, because awareness is your first line of defense.

Why Do We Act Like This?

I didn't study behavioral science, but after two decades in heels, armed with lipstick and a front-row seat to corporate chaos, I've got a theory that's 90% stand-up comedy, 10% people-watching, and 100% earned from coaching women through the mess.

Let's briefly entertain this theory: Back in prehistoric human days, there were fewer men than women, which meant women had to compete, loudly and visibly, to secure a mate. Fast-forward a few thousand years, and we're still doing it. Only now it's not about firewood and cave space; it's about recognition, influence, and professional power.

The competition hasn't gone away; it's just wearing a pantsuit.

You can see it in any environment where resources feel scarce, whether that's funding, recognition, mentorship, or access. When women feel like there's only room for one of us at the top, we don't band together, we push each other off the ladder. And that's the behavior we must dismantle.

Here's the Good News

Once you see the patterns, you can stop participating. Instead, you can:

- Praise another woman in a meeting.
- Loop her into an email thread.
- Recommend her for the opportunity you don't want.
- Choose collaboration over competition, even when it's hard.

No one's saying you must be best friends with every woman you work with. Friendship isn't required. But being kind, fair, and supportive doesn't cost a thing, and it makes a difference every single time you do it. Think of it like holding the door open for someone - it takes almost no effort, but it changes how that person feels in the moment. In the workplace, when you choose to act as an ally, you're not just helping one person, you're showing everyone around you what respect and teamwork look like.

Example of Allyship in Action

At a former job, a junior employee shared a bold idea during a strategy session. She spoke up with courage, but at first her suggestion was met with silence. That could have been the end of it. But then a senior woman spoke up and said, "Let's circle back to that idea. I think she's onto something." Suddenly, the idea that might have been ignored got a second chance, and the whole room began to take it seriously.

This is allyship at work. The senior woman didn't take over the idea, and she didn't try to make herself the center of attention. She simply used her voice and her position to make sure someone else's voice was heard. That one sentence shifted the tone of the meeting.

Yes, Even the "Nice" Ones

You might be thinking, "But I'm not like that!" Really? Let's check yourself. Have you ever:

- Judged another woman's outfit, hair, or voice?
- Felt low-key irritated when someone younger gets praise?
- Wanted to roll your eyes when a new hire came in too confident?

We all have. The difference? Some of us correct ourselves. Others let the behavior set up shop in their soul. Catching yourself in these moments doesn't make you a bad colleague, it makes you human. The growth comes in choosing differently the next time.

This chapter isn't about blame, it's about awareness. You can't change what you won't acknowledge.

Coming Up Next

You're about to reflect on your own experiences with female competition and judgment in the next section. Whether you've just joined the workforce or you've already navigated your fair share of office politics, the *Judged by the Cover* worksheet will help you unpack where these dynamics have shown up in your life.

It might sting a little. But that's okay because that's the start of change.

The sabotage may wear heels, but so do you. Yours are made for breaking patterns, not just walking hallways. Let's start by defining your path, before the culture tries to shape it for you.

Judged by the Cover

Before you join the breakroom drama, let's do some self-reflecting. Think about your own girl-code slip-ups: eye rolls, silent treatment, or judging Janet's shoes. This worksheet isn't about blame; it's your revelation to do better.

1. Think of a time a woman made you feel:
(check all that apply)
- [ ] Supported
- [ ] Inspired
- [ ] Judged
- [ ] Sabotaged
- [ ] Ignored
- [ ] Intimidated
- [ ] Protected
- [ ] Left out
- [ ] Like a threat
- [ ] Like you belonged

Which one shows up most often for you? Circle it.

2. Now, write about one experience that still sticks with you:
- *Who was involved (no names needed)? • What happened? • How did it make you feel?*

3. Have *you* ever felt judgmental, threatened, or competitive with another woman? Be honest!
- *What triggered it? • Was it her confidence? Her title? Her outfit? Her energy?*

4. What do you want to do differently moving forward?
- *How will you show up with more awareness, support, or intention for other women?*

WHO BUILT THE CULTURE

Just because someone's been in the workplace longer doesn't automatically make them better: Seniority ≠ Superiority. But it *does* mean they've had more time to shape the workplace you're now stepping into. If you want to change culture, you must understand the two generations of women who've been running the show: Baby Boomers and Generation X.

They're not just older co-workers; they're the cultural architects of the environment you're walking into. The blueprint may be outdated, but it's the one you'll have to navigate.

What This Chapter *Won't* Do

This isn't a sociology lecture. We're not reviewing buzzword-heavy infographics about generational mindsets. If you want to read about "digital natives," "resilience," and "grit," Google has you covered.

This chapter is about what it's *really* like to work with Baby Boomers and Gen X women; the unfiltered version you won't find in HR training or LinkedIn think pieces.

Why Focus on These Two Generations?

It's not because Millennials and Gen Z don't matter; you are the future of the workforce. But, if we're going to break harmful cycles, we need to look up the ladder, not just across. Boomers and Gen X women are still in charge in many organizations. If we're going to shift the culture, we first must understand what shaped theirs.

Quick Word of Warning:

Do **NOT** march into a work environment and start diagnosing your co-workers as "Boomer Burnouts" or "Gen X Helicopter Rebels." If you do, you'll find yourself in HR faster than you can say "generational trauma." This chapter is about insight, not ammunition.

Read it and remember it. And when you find yourself whispering, *"What is even happening right now?"* you'll have some answers.

Meet the Generations Shaping Today's Workplace

Baby Boomers (Ages 60–78)

Historical Context:

These women entered a workplace that wasn't just male-dominated, it was male-defined. They dealt with sexism, inappropriate comments, and being expected to fetch coffee while crushing it in their roles. Many fought like hell for the rights you now enjoy - maternity leave, harassment policies, flexible schedules, and leadership pipelines for women.

Workplace Traits:

1. **The Armor of Survival.**

Many Boomer women climbed the ladder old-school: stay long, work hard, and prove yourself. They endured sexism and silence, and in the process internalized harmful norms like perfectionism, hierarchy, and competition. The armor they wear today isn't always cruelty, often it's the residue of survival.

2. **Intimidating, but not cold.**

These women are usually in leadership. They move fast and speak directly. They don't do fluff. You'll hear them described as "tough," "unapproachable," or "intense." But if you earn their trust, you'll find wisdom, loyalty, and a genuine desire to help younger women succeed.

3. **Counting the days.**

Ask any Baby Boomer when they're retiring and they'll tell you down to the exact day. Many are hanging on for one reason: Medicare. They're not trying to build empires; they're trying to make it to the finish line. Of course, this isn't every Boomer woman's story, but it's a pattern I've seen repeatedly in my HR career, especially among those who've weathered decades of workplace battles. Their perspective often reflects survival, not disengagement.

Bottom line: They've earned their rest. But if they check out too early, they leave you without a map, or worse, with a broken one.

Generation X (Ages 44–59)

Historical Context:

These are the latchkey kids who turned into corporate warriors. They grew up letting themselves into the house, microwaving dinner, and figuring life out while their parents worked late. Their childhoods bred independence, skepticism, and a deep distrust of authority. Now they're your boss.

Workplace Traits:

1. **Ruthless efficiency.**

   Gen X women get it done. They don't wait for permission, they don't coddle co-workers, and they don't have time for incompetence. If you get in their way, they will go around you, and they won't apologize.

2. **They intimidate men. Seriously.**

These women have navigated boys' club boardrooms with sharp heels and sharper opinions. Are there studies proving this? Nope. Just decades of whispered boardroom dynamics, unspoken avoidance, and male colleagues tiptoeing around them.

3. **Busy is their baseline.**

If a Gen X woman isn't multitasking fourteen things at once, she's not okay. Idle time makes her restless. She'll either job hop, start a side hustle, or start drama. For you, that means learning to respect her pace but also setting boundaries, so you're not pulled into constant overdrive. And yes, I'll admit, I fit this description myself. Not every Gen X woman will, but in my experience many of us were raised to equate productivity with value. What looks like restlessness is often a survival skill we never learned to turn off.

Bottom line: Gen X women aren't here to impress you. But if you can earn their respect? You've got an unshakable ally.

Of course, my generational descriptions aren't absolute; they're patterns I've observed in my HR career. While not every woman will fit them, they might show up often enough to influence the culture you're walking into.

Why This Matters to You

If you understand where these women come from, you'll understand why they're often:

- Dismissive of your enthusiasm.
- Critical of your new ideas.
- Cold when you're craving connection.

They're not always being mean. They're being shaped by experiences, survival, and generations of working twice as hard for half the recognition. But just because that's the system they inherited doesn't mean you have to accept it. You get to learn from it and then choose differently.

When Generations Clash, It Gets Messy, Fast

When Boomer and Gen X women clash, it can escalate quickly. Power struggles, dismissiveness, and ego flare-ups may happen behind closed doors, but the tension seeps into every meeting, email, and hallway interaction. The smallest disagreement can spiral into an "us vs. them" standoff.

Why? Because both sides are convinced, they're right and neither wants to compromise. I've seen entire teams fall apart because two generational leaders refused to collaborate.

Here are just a few examples I've witnessed:
- A Gen X manager undermines a Boomer counterpart by looping in higher-ups behind her back.
- A Boomer team lead shuts down every suggestion from her Gen X colleague with a patronizing, "We've tried that before."
- A passive-aggressive email sparks a reply-all war that leaves the whole team on edge.
- Two senior women openly compete for influence, dragging others into whispered alliances and public callouts.
- Constant finger-pointing to leadership, with repeated attempts to get the other person fired.

Now imagine being the youngest voice in that room. You're not dismissed because you lack ability, but because you haven't yet been accepted as part of either "team." For younger employees, this clash can show up as mixed messages; one leader demanding endless documentation, while another dismisses your reports as overkill.

How to Survive the Clash

If you're new and eager to prove yourself, beware of being recruited to a side. It won't look like sabotage; it'll be disguised as support. Flattery, whispered warnings, "just so you know" gossip, these are tactics used to discredit the other side and gain your loyalty. Don't mistake it for being chosen. They're not looking for protégés, they're looking for backup.

Survival Strategies

You won't be able to stop the clash, but you can avoid becoming collateral damage. Here's how to protect your reputation and stay focused on what really matters:

1. **Know When to Speak and When to Watch.**
   Sometimes the smartest move is to observe and learn the players before stepping in.
2. **Don't Take It Personally, Even When It Feels Personal.**
   Their reactions often stem from insecurities. Your confidence may trigger what they were once told to suppress.
3. **Document Everything.**
   Track your work, your contributions, and any significant communication. In a culture shaped by hierarchy and politics, your credibility depends on receipts, not assumptions.
4. **Stay Professional, Not Passive.**
   Respect doesn't mean silence. Set boundaries with clarity and confidence. Being

quiet won't protect your reputation, but poise will.
5. **Build Strategic Relationships.**
Find at least one person in each generation who can offer insight. You don't need best friends, you need perspective, access, and support.
6. **Protect Your Energy.**
Not every jab deserves a reaction. Save your energy for the work that builds your credibility, not the drama that drains it.

Bridging the Generational Divide

Understanding the dynamics between Boomer and Gen X women isn't about picking sides, it's about recognizing how generational values, leadership styles, and unspoken hierarchies shape the workplace you're stepping into. These tensions don't exist because women don't want to support one another, but because unresolved history and hard-earned survival tactics still linger beneath the surface.

Your role isn't to shrink or stay silent; it's to see the bigger picture and respond with strategy instead of self-doubt, so you don't inherit their survival tactics.

You've seen how the blueprint was built and how it still shows up. Now it's your turn: test your awareness through a scenario that mirrors what you may soon face.

Case Study: Why Those Women Hate You

Generational Tension in the Workplace
Meet Taylor, a 25-year-old new hire in a mid-sized marketing firm. She's smart, motivated, and full of fresh ideas. She graduated top of her class, completed a successful internship program, and walked into her new job ready to make an impact. Her enthusiasm wasn't fake, it was fueled by years of being told to "use your voice," "be confident," and "make change happen." But within her first month, Taylor felt the air shift. Conversations that once seemed welcoming grew colder. Ideas that once earned nods now drew interruptions. And the confidence she'd been praised for in school was suddenly being treated as arrogance in the workplace.

By the third month, she stopped volunteering ideas in meetings. By the fourth month, she dreaded walking into the office. Lisa, a Baby Boomer VP, rarely let Taylor finish a full thought. Instead, she interrupted, redirected the conversation, and then resurfaced Taylor's ideas later as if they were her own. Gina, a Gen X manager, added to the tension, muttering more than once that Taylor was "too confident for someone with no experience." And when Taylor pitched a new project, the response was a dismissive, "Let's not reinvent the wheel."

The shift was subtle but steady, and Taylor began to question herself. Was she being too much? Had she overstepped? Or was something else at play?

What's Really Happening
Lisa and Gina weren't trying to be cruel, but they were reacting through the lens of their own battles. Lisa had clawed her way into leadership in a world that silenced women. Gina had built credibility by being twice as competent and half as emotional as her male peers. Taylor? She represented a new playbook: a generation encouraged to be vocal, confident, and unapologetic. Her presence wasn't disrespectful, but it triggered old insecurities in others. Taylor wasn't the problem. But how she handled it would define her next chapter.

The Lesson
When women from different generations clash, it's often about history, not personality. Taylor didn't need to dim her light, she needed strategy. Documenting her work, seeking cross-generational allies, and framing her ideas as collaborations instead of disruptions can help her build credibility without shrinking. And Lisa and Gina?

They also have an opportunity: to notice when old scars are shaping new judgments and choose to lead differently.

Reflection Questions:

1. If you were Taylor, what specific steps could you take to protect your confidence while still respecting Lisa and Gina's experience?

2. Have you ever been on either side of this experience as the newcomer doubting yourself or the seasoned professional feeling protective of your turf?

3. What strategies from this chapter (documentation, boundaries, building allies) could help bridge generational gaps without sacrificing authenticity?

4. Have you ever unintentionally reacted to a younger colleague's confidence because it reminded you of your own struggles? How might you choose differently next time?

5. How can you lead yourself in spaces where generational tension is unspoken but clearly present?

Reminder: The goal isn't to shrink, but to strategize. Generational dynamics don't have to define you but understanding them gives you the edge to navigate with confidence.

PERCEPTION IS REALITY

You Don't Get to Pick Your Reputation, But You Can Learn to Shape It

A colleague once asked why a young woman didn't get promoted. The answer? "She just doesn't seem ready." When pressed to explain what "ready" meant, no one could define it. There were no performance issues, no negative feedback, just a vague impression that she wasn't quite "there yet." She didn't get passed over because of her work ethic, she got passed over because of perception. And that's the dangerous part: perception doesn't have to be rooted in reality to rewrite your career story.

When others think you're too quiet, too bold, too confident, too something, you can find yourself sidelined without ever being told why. That's why this chapter exists: if you don't take control of how you show up, someone else's assumptions will do it for you.

We've talked about the workplace power players, Boomers and Gen X, and how their unspoken rules still run the show. Now it's time to flip the script. The next power move is not just understanding them, it's understanding how they see you and why that perception matters more than you'd like.

Let's Get Real About This

We already talked about the ugly truth: you may not be liked the second you show up. You won't get a welcome mat; you'll get a microscope. How you look, speak, and carry yourself under that microscope can decide whether you're seen as a rising star or a threat that needs managing.

In the workplace, perception *IS* reality. You don't have to do anything *wrong* to trigger a negative reaction, you just have to exist outside someone else's comfort zone. It doesn't matter what your intentions are, it's how your actions, attitude, and presence are *interpreted* by the people around you. Especially by women who came before you and have a completely different rulebook.

💬 *You could be showing up as "motivated and prepared," but to someone else, that looks like "cocky and trying too hard." You think you're just being yourself. They think you're trying to take their spot."*

Early on, you'll need to be extra intentional, so your competence cuts through the noise of perception.

The Double Standard Dilemma

This whole dynamic wouldn't be happening if the playing field were level. But it's not.

- A Gen X woman who's blunt? She's called "direct."
- A younger woman who's blunt? She's called "disrespectful."
- A Boomer who says she's too busy to help? "She's a leader with priorities."
- A Millennial who sets boundaries? "She's lazy or not a team player."

Same behavior. Different generations. Wildly different consequences.

One young woman I coached was told she was "immature" for pushing back on unrealistic deadlines. Meanwhile, her Gen X boss called the same behavior in herself "managing expectations." Same action. Different labels. Different power.

You're not just dealing with perception, you're dealing with decades of unspoken rules, invisible tension, and emotional landmines. But if you can understand how you're being perceived, you can start to shift the narrative.

When Appearance Becomes a Red Flag

Let's not kid ourselves, workplaces absolutely judge people, especially women, based on how they look. And it gets real personal, fast. You might think you're being evaluated on your talent or potential, but often it starts with your heels, your hair, or whether you wore lipstick to the staff meeting.

Women size each other up over makeup choices, bra straps, baby weight, resting face, vocal tone, and even lunch orders. One glance and the verdict's already in. This chapter isn't about vanity, it's about awareness. If you want to play the game and still own your look, you must know the rules you're up against and how to navigate them strategically.

From Tattoos to Textures: What They Really See

Sadly, I've seen women judged for tattoos and piercings. What's meant to be self-expression often gets twisted into questions of "professionalism." A wrist tattoo peeking out of a jacket or a nose ring in a client meeting shouldn't define your credibility, but for some, it does. These judgments aren't really about ink or jewelry; they're about bias.

That same bias runs even deeper when it comes to racial and cultural identity markers, like natural hairstyles, braids, or head coverings. Too often, these choices aren't viewed as professional, and they're labeled as distractions or even defiance.

That's not about workplace standards, it's about stereotypes. And when bias shows up at that level, it doesn't just question your style. It questions your place at the table.

Whether it's a tattoo, a nose ring, or the way you wear your hair, what's really being judged isn't style, it's conformity. The moment you recognize that, it stops feeling personal and starts revealing itself for what it is: bias.

But I'm Just Being Me...

You should be yourself. But here's the truth: the world doesn't read intentions, it reads impact. That doesn't mean conforming, it means showing up with enough self-awareness to steer how your story gets told.

When you understand how others perceive you, you gain the power to:
- Redirect false narratives.
- Build strategic relationships
- Avoid unnecessary battles.
- Make intentional, not reactive, choices.

Perception shapes your professional path, so instead of playing defense, learn to direct the story. You're not there to win a popularity contest; you're there to deliver results and build your career.

That starts by knowing the game you're stepping into, heels first, head high. By predicting how others might misread you, you can adjust how you show up, not to please them, but to protect your power.

How do you do that? By making a conscious effort to communicate with clarity, set boundaries early, and carry yourself with consistency, even when you're underestimated.

Intersectionality Matters

Workplace culture doesn't land evenly on everyone's shoulders. The unwritten rules of "how things are done" often come with invisible barriers that hit some groups harder than others. Neurodivergent women may be unfairly judged as "awkward" or "difficult" simply because their communication style doesn't mirror the norm. LGBTQ+ professionals may be sidelined with the vague critique of not being a "culture fit"—a phrase that often disguises bias. And first-generation professionals from lower socioeconomic backgrounds may constantly feel a step behind, not because of their ability, but because no one ever taught them the silent codes of office life that others take for granted.

To be a true culture breaker is to recognize these inequities and actively dismantle them. It means creating space where every woman—regardless of how she looks, thinks, or where she comes from—has a seat at the table and the confidence that her contributions matter. Culture breaking is not about assimilation; it's about expanding the definition of belonging.

The Harsh Truth

No matter how strong your skills are, your career path will often be shaped by how other women perceive you. That's why it's essential to understand these dynamics and learn how to navigate them with clarity and confidence.

Worksheet: How Are You Being Perceived?

The next page is where it gets personal. Think of it as your perception profile. You'll practice seeing yourself the way others might. Not to change who you are, but to sharpen how you lead your story.

Remember, this isn't about shame. It's about strategy. Because when you understand perception, you stop being defined by it and start directing it.

Self-Perception Profile

Perception is power. You don't get to control the first draft of your reputation, but you do get to edit it. This worksheet is your mirror and your megaphone. Be real, be unfiltered, and get ready to shape the story before someone else writes it for you.

Step 1: First Impressions - *The Snap Judgment Test*
Think about how you show up on a typical day. What are the first three things' people notice about you (before you even open your laptop)?
1. _____
2. _____
3. _____

Now ask yourself:
What snap assumptions might someone make based on those three things alone?

_____
_____
_____

Step 2: What's Your Look Saying Before You Even Talk?
Let's be real: your appearance sends a message, whether you mean it to or not. Check anything that fits your usual vibe:

- [ ] Visible tattoos
- [ ] Facial piercings
- [ ] Bright/dyed hair
- [ ] Natural or textured hairstyle
- [ ] Braids, locs, or twists
- [ ] Minimalist look
- [ ] Designer style
- [ ] Business casual
- [ ] Bold makeup
- [ ] No makeup
- [ ] Loud accessories
- [ ] Corporate sleek
- [ ] Cultural attire

Now reflect:
If someone 15+ years older than you met you today, what might your look be telling them — fair or not?

Step 3: How Does Your Voice Come Across?
Your words matter, but so does the way you deliver them. Circle what fits you best:
- **Tone:** Friendly / Direct / Reserved / Assertive / Casual
- **Volume:** Quiet / Medium / Loud
- **Style:** Collaborative / Independent / Inquisitive / Straightforward

Now dig deeper:
What could someone misunderstand about the way you speak or interact?

_____
_____

And what do you want your communication to say about you?

_____
_____

Bonus check: How do you want people to **feel** after talking to you?

_____

Step 4: Reality vs. Intention — *The Misunderstanding Audit*
Think of a time you were misunderstood.
- What happened?
- How were you perceived?
- What was your actual intention?

_____
_____

Now flip it:
If you could do it again, what would you do differently to make sure your impact matched your intention?

_____
_____

Step 5: Rewrite the Narrative — *Own Your Word*
If perception is power, this is where you take it back.
- What **ONE word** do you want people to walk away with after meeting you?

   _____

- What is **one action** you can take (consistently, not once) to reinforce that word until people start saying it about you?

   _____

DON'T WEAPONIZE YOUR INSECURITIES

What if the biggest threat to surviving the workplace isn't sexism, bias, or bad policy, but unchecked insecurity? Not the kind you whisper about in a journal, but the kind that leaks out in your tone, your body language, and the way you treat the next woman who walks through the door.

Why It Matters

Unacknowledged insecurity becomes sabotage. The more you own your inner mess, the less likely you are to make someone else pay for it. Everyone in the workplace has insecurities. No one is immune. The woman in the sharp blazer who talks like she owns the building, or your manager who seems like she's never doubted herself a day in her life. Yes, even the VP who throws around buzzwords like she invented the concept of strategy. The difference? They've just gotten better at hiding it.

Here's what no one tells you: while you may be walking in terrified that you don't belong, they may be looking at you wondering how long until you take their seat. They see your energy, education, ease with technology, and fresh ideas and it shakes them. Not because they don't want you to succeed, but because your rise reminds them of their own limits. If they haven't dealt with their insecurities, you'll feel their resentment before you've even figured out where the bathroom is.

You don't grow up in a world full of unrealistic expectations, curated comparisons, and constant judgment without absorbing a few fears of your own. And neither did they. But here's the kicker: what you don't acknowledge will end up running the show. And it won't run it quietly. It will:

- Show up as defensiveness in feedback.
- Drive competition instead of collaboration.
- Turn small stressors into big culture problems.
- Leak into meetings, reviews, and hallway conversations.

Unchecked insecurity doesn't just sit quietly in the background. It drives behavior, culture, and careers, unless you stop it.

If You Don't Own It, It Owns You

We all have that one "thing" we secretly hope no one notices. Maybe you're afraid of speaking up in meetings because you don't want to sound stupid; or you're terrified someone will realize you're not as qualified as your résumé makes you look; or maybe you fear your background, your accent, or your upbringing makes you seem "less professional." Whatever it is, if you don't name it, it will start making decisions for you. You'll shrink in meetings, second-guess your ideas, or overwork yourself into exhaustion trying to "prove" you belong. You'll play small, or you'll play too tough, and both are just fear wearing different outfits.

If you don't deal with it? One of two things usually happens:

Option 1: You Burn Out

When you walk into a job trying to prove you're not insecure, it shows, and not in the way you hope. You'll say yes to everything, stay later than everyone else, and bend over backward to outperform your team. Not because it's strategy, but because you're scared of being "found out."

That's when imposter syndrome digs in. You stop asking questions and you stop setting boundaries. Suddenly, you're living at the office, stressed out, and wondering why your dream job feels like punishment. Burnout doesn't just come from workload. It comes from hiding who you really are.

Option 2: You Become Them

Here's the hard truth: if you don't heal what hurt you, you'll hand that pain to the next woman who walks through the door.

It starts small. You get annoyed at the new hire because she's a little too confident. You roll your eyes when she asks the questions you once were too afraid to ask. You'll judge her outfit, her tone, her ambition, and you will justify it because: "Someone needs to humble her."

Sound familiar? That's how generational oppression works: woman to woman, not just boss to employee. You become a gatekeeper by criticizing instead of mentoring and tearing down instead of building up. Not because you're cruel, but because you're still wounded.

💬 *Unacknowledged insecurity doesn't just hold you back. It reshapes the entire culture around you.*

Hurt People Gatekeep

Gatekeeping is when someone hoards access, knowledge, or opportunity under the illusion of "standards" or "earning your stripes." It's subtle, but the results are the same: exclusion, stalling, and lost potential.

Examples?
- Intentionally leaving someone out of a meeting they should be in.
- Hoarding information that would make someone else's job easier.
- Promotion criteria shifting the moment you get close.
- A senior colleague who could clear your path but instead blocks it with "she's not ready yet."

Here's the truth: you're not more legitimate because you suffered. The next woman doesn't have to bleed just because you did.

When Their Insecurities Almost Became Mine

I once worked with two women in executive roles who looked polished and powerful on paper. Behind closed doors? Their insecurities were driving the bus.

One carried shame over not having a degree. The other carried abandonment wounds from her father (her words, not mine). Both wore heels and titles, but what they really carried into every meeting was pain they hadn't faced.

Instead of owning it, they projected it. They siloed departments, spread gossip, and pulled me into their crossfire. Each whispered their side and angled for my loyalty. And when I stayed neutral? They turned on me, twisting the story to make me look disloyal.

That's what happens when you're surrounded by people who haven't dealt with their insecurities: they weaponize relationships, twist perceptions, and leave you doubting yourself. If you don't own your insecurities, someone else's will. And when their fear runs the room, it can quietly rewrite your path, your confidence, and your future.

It's Okay to Have Insecurities — It's Not Okay to Weaponize Them

You're allowed to feel unsure, to question yourself, to wonder if you're in over your head. What you're not allowed to do is punish the women around you because they reflect the parts of you that still feel unworthy.

Sometimes, insecurities don't even start at work. They come from the baggage you drag through the front door. I once worked with a woman whose husband tore her down daily at home. She had no power there, so she clung to it at the office. Her insecurity wasn't about performance; it was about self-worth. And how did she cope? By controlling and belittling others. That's how cycles form. That's why this work matters.

Allow Yourself to Feel Stupid

Yes, you read that right. You're going to feel stupid. And that's okay. If you've never felt stupid in your first 30 days on the job, you probably weren't trained right.

Here's the truth: you are not supposed to know everything right away. You are not Google. You are human. Six months — that's about how long it takes to really understand your role, the systems, the people, and the politics.

So, give yourself grace in month one. Patience in month two. By month six? That's when you can decide if this role is right for you, not before. Survival isn't about being perfect fast, it's about lasting long enough to learn.

Break the Pattern Before You Repeat It

The workplace doesn't need more women climbing ladders just to yank them up behind them. It doesn't need more managers who demand perfection but offer no support. What it does need is women brave enough to ask: Am I showing up with clarity, or am I letting fear run the show?

Because here's the legacy check: You didn't fight to get in the room just to become the kind of woman someone else can't wait to escape.

Clarity Starts Here

Before you turn the page, breathe. The *What's Really Driving You Worksheet* that follows isn't busy work; it's a chance to pause and name what's really underneath your choices.

Do it now, while it's quiet. Because if you don't know what's driving you, you'll end up being driven by insecurity, fear, and the approval of people who don't pay your bills.

You don't have to be fearless to survive in the workplace. You just have to be self-aware enough not to turn your fears into someone else's scars.

What's Really Driving You?

The parts of you that whisper "not enough" will always find a mic. Sometimes it's in your words, sometimes in your silence, and sometimes in the eye roll you don't mean to give. The goal isn't to erase them — it's to make sure fear isn't the one running your career.

Step 1: Name It to Tame It:
Everybody's got an "I'm not enough" tape playing in the background. Yours might sound different, but it's still there. The first step is hitting pause long enough to hear it.

What are you most afraid people will think about you? *(Choose as many as apply or add your own.)*

- ☐ I'm not qualified enough
- ☐ I'm too young
- ☐ I'm too old
- ☐ I'm not pretty enough
- ☐ I'm not smart enough
- ☐ I'm too quiet
- ☐ I'm too loud
- ☐ I don't fit in
- ☐ I don't look the part
- ☐ I'll never be taken seriously
- ☐ I'll mess it up
- ☐ I'm not as good as they think I am (Imposter Syndrome)
- ☐ I'll be replaced
- ☐ _____
- ☐ _____

Step 2: Track the Trigger
Insecurity isn't random, it has patterns. Think about the last time yours flared up. What set it off? Who was involved? And how did it change how you showed up?

Describe the moment:

_____
_____
_____
_____

Step 3: What's the Real Story?
Fear tells stories that facts can't back up. Look at that moment again: what part was real, and what part was your insecurity playing narrator?

Reflection:
_____
_____

Step 4: Create a Grounding Statement
This is your comeback line to yourself — the one that shuts insecurity down before it takes the wheel.
Example: "I was hired because I bring value, not because I'm perfect."
Example: "Not knowing something doesn't make me unqualified. It makes me teachable."

Your grounding truth:
_____
_____
_____

Step 5: Build Your Plan
Insecurity will show up again, that's a guarantee. The difference is whether you spiral or have a survival move ready.

Pick one go-to action for the next time it tries to take over.
- [ ] Take a walk before responding
- [ ] Write (but don't send) the email
- [ ] Talk to someone I trust
- [ ] Remind myself of my grounding statement
- [ ] Pause and ask: "What's really happening here?"
- [ ] Other: _____

What kind of woman do you want to be when someone else's insecurity walks into the room?
_____
_____
_____

MISTAKES WILL BE MAGNIFIED

What if I told you the mistake itself isn't the problem; it's the spotlight that follows? In a workplace shaped by competition and insecurity, your slip-ups don't just land, they echo.

You're going to fail. Not because you're careless or secretly terrible at your job, but because you're human, navigating a flawed, fast-moving system. You'll:
- Miss something obvious.
- Misread the room.
- Send the wrong file.
- Speak too fast, or not at all.
- Forget to CC your boss and, yes, even send something to your ex instead of your team.

The truth? Failure is guaranteed. What matters is how you handle it because that response, not the mistake, will define your credibility.

Failure Isn't the End. It's the Beginning.

If you were raised to believe your worth comes from never messing up, buckle up. The workplace doesn't reward perfection; it rewards progress. And nothing accelerates progress like falling flat on your face.

Every woman you admire? She's failed more times than you can count. You just don't hear about it because we glamorize the win and erase the process.

Failure forces three things:
1. **Clarity.** Gaps get exposed, and knowledge fills in fast.
2. **Resilience.** The test is whether the fall knocks you out or fuels your return.
3. **Humility.** Failure reminds us no one is the exception.

The goal isn't to avoid failure. The goal is to fail better, smarter, faster, and with enough emotional maturity to take the hit and still hold your head high.

Perfection builds ego. Failure builds character.

The Double Standard No One Warns You About

Here's the complication: in workplaces where women are often competing for space, failure isn't just seen as "learning." It's seen as leverage. That typo in your email? Someone will casually forward it to your boss. That fumble in the meeting? Expect to hear it echoed back two weeks later as a "reminder." Why? Because your mistake is their opportunity. If they haven't done the inner work, your slip-up becomes their steppingstone.

And the irony? When they mess up, it disappears into silent PR crisis mode - minimized, buried, and daring anyone to bring it up. It's not sabotage with knives, it's sabotage with whispers, screenshots, and selective memory.

Two Rules That Will Save You

Rule 1: Own It Before They Do:

If you mess up - and you will - don't wait for the rumor mill to spin. Say it first: *"I made a mistake. Here's what I'm doing to fix it."* Eleven words that kill gossip before it grows. People don't need flawless; they need accountable.

Rule 2: Don't Let Their Insecurity Amplify Yours

When someone magnifies your mistake, it's tempting to shrink. That's the trap. If you spiral in doubt, you're no longer competing, you're sidelined. Use failure as fuel. Learn. Adjust. Then show up stronger.

Own it. Refuse it. Use it. That's the cycle-breaker.

Real Talk Example: The Rookie and the Leader

A young woman I coached - brand new, fresh out of school, smart - was tasked with pulling data for a client report headed straight to leadership. She did everything right... except for one column she forgot to update.

By the time it was caught, the report had already made the rounds. Panic? Of course. But instead of hiding, she flagged it herself, apologized without excuses, corrected it, and re-sent it with three bullet points on how she'd prevent it next time.

Result? No one held it against her. In fact, her credibility grew. Why? Because she did what most professionals twice her age still avoid - she owned it.

Now compare that to a senior manager I once worked with. Impressive title. Solid résumé. But when deadlines slipped, she blamed the team. When deliverables failed, she claimed she "wasn't looped in." When cornered, she got defensive or threw someone else under the bus. It wasn't the mistakes that destroyed her reputation. It was the cover-ups. Over time, no one trusted her. People documented every interaction with her "just in case."

💬 *The lesson: Failure doesn't ruin you. The denial does.*

Final Thought: You Can Fail and Still Belong

Let's break the myth that one mistake disqualifies you. You're going to screw up. Expect it. Plan for it. But never let it convince you you're unworthy. The real test isn't avoiding failure. It's being able to say: *"I messed up… and I'm still capable, still valuable, and still here."* That's how you survive in a culture quick to magnify your flaws: not by dodging every misstep, but by refusing to let failure be the final word.

The mistake doesn't define you. The recovery does.

A+ STUDENT DOESN'T MEAN A+ PROFESSIONAL

You studied. You aced finals. You survived group projects with slackers. But none of that prepared you for the hardest test of your career: other women. And guess what? Everyone, whether they hold a college degree or a high school diploma, starts off on the same emotional playing field.

Now before the academic overachievers start hyperventilating, let me clarify: Yes, certain degrees will give you a technical edge. And yes, some fields (hello, neurosurgery) absolutely require academic mastery. But in most professional environments - where people send too many emails, instant messages that feel like more like cryptic Morse code, and team meetings that might as well be improv comedy nights - you'll quickly learn that what gets you ahead has less to do with textbook knowledge and more to do with your people skills.

You Can't Learn Office Politics from a Syllabus

School taught you how to write essays, calculate equations, and regurgitate facts on command. What they didn't teach you:

- How to navigate a team full of insecure co-workers.
- Decode passive-aggressive emails.
- Spot the subtle way your boss takes credit for your idea and calls it 'collaboration.'
- Sit through a meeting where two women pretend to be besties and then go whisper about each other in the breakroom.

The skills you *actually* need to succeed - emotional intelligence, boundary setting, conflict resolution - are nowhere to be found in a classroom. You're not reading this book because school gave you all the answers. You're reading it because you've already sensed something isn't quite right or you've had a female figure in your life complain about working with other women.

Why Nobody Talks About It

Here's a theory I've been sitting on for years, and I'm only half joking: maybe the reason no one warns us about how hard it is to work with other women is because if they had, half of us would've peaced out before even applying for our first job. Imagine sitting in a college seminar and hearing this:

"By the way, a big part of your career success will depend on navigating subtle competition, underhanded sabotage, and emotional tension with women who should be supporting you."

Yeah… hard pass.

But here's the wild part: what if the silence wasn't just ignorance? what if it's by design?

Let me toss out a theory for your consideration (cue conspiracy music):

- What if the division between women is exactly what "the man" wants?
- What if the unspoken competition, the gossip, the gatekeeping, and the silent sabotage we're so used to… isn't just a byproduct of workplace culture, but part of the plan?

Think about it. If women stay too busy fighting each other, we don't rise together. If we keep circling in jealousy and comparison, we don't collaborate and we keep burning out, opting out, or selling out – and guess who still runs the show? Not us.

Boom! Conspiracy complete. It's almost believable, right?

But here's the truth: we don't need a conspiracy theory to explain bad behavior. We just need awareness, because *most* of this comes from one thing: women entering the workplace without being told what they were actually walking into. That's what this book is here to change.

Now that you know the dynamics - the pressures, projections, and power struggles - you get to show up differently.

You don't have to become another woman who silences, sabotages, or competes in secret and you don't have to play the old games or pass down the pains, because you have something they didn't: clarity.

And clarity doesn't just protect your peace, it makes you a threat to the system, because you won't be repeating it. So, the question becomes: will you play along, or will you break the pattern?

Breaking the Cycle

If we're going to break the cycle, we must name what's fueling it. The truth is, not every woman will root for you, and sometimes, you might even catch yourself slipping into judgment, comparison, or silence. That doesn't make you the villain. It makes you human. What matters is what you do next.

The next page is a reflection worksheet to help you build awareness so you can walk into any room as a woman who chooses support over sabotage. Let's take a hard look inward, so you can show up with purpose.

Why Don't Women Always Support Other Women?

Before we can break the cycle, we've got to stop pretending it doesn't exist. This worksheet is your mirror - time to face the messy truth about female competition, silence, and support.

1. **Quick Gut Check**

In your opinion, what are the *top 3 reasons* some women don't support other women in the workplace? (There's no wrong answer - only your truth.)
- ☐ Insecurity
- ☐ Fear of being replaced
- ☐ Competition for limited leadership roles
- ☐ Personal bias or jealousy
- ☐ Lack of positive female role models
- ☐ Generational divide
- ☐ Poor past experiences with women
- ☐ Toxic company culture
- ☐ It's just how they were taught to survive
- ☐ Other: _____

2. **Rate Your Experience**

How often have *you* felt unsupported by other women?
(1 = Never (lucky unicorn); 3 = Sometimes (welcome to the club); 5 = Constantly (you've got stories that deserve wine + therapy)

[1] [2] [3] [4] [5]

How often have you *seen* other women being unsupportive of each other?
[1] [2] [3] [4] [5]

3. **Let's Get Real**

Have you ever judged, dismissed, or competed with another woman before really getting to know her? Honesty matters here, because awareness is the only way to stop playing the same tired game

☐ Yes

☐ No

☐ If I'm being honest... probably.

What was driving that reaction? (Be brave. Be honest.)
→ _____
→ _____

→ _____

4. What Support *Looks* Like
Think about a woman who made you feel seen, supported, or empowered. What did she *do* that made the difference?
→ _____
→ _____
→ _____

Now flip it, how can *you* show up like that for someone else?
→ _____
→ _____
→ _____

5. Your Accountability Reminder
Complete this sentence:
"I want to be the kind of woman who _____ instead of the kind of woman who _____."

Example: "I want to be a woman who invites others in instead of *hoarding opportunities."*

6. Make a Move, Not Just a Statement
What's *one specific action* you can make to support another woman instead of silently competing with or judging her?
→ _____
→ _____
→ _____
→ _____

Need inspiration? Supporting another woman can be as simple as mentoring, making a referral, celebrating her win, or choosing kindness over criticism.

NO ONE'S TOSSING A LIFE RAFT

A new hire once told me, *"I kept waiting for someone to explain what to do. But no one did, so I just kept failing."* Unfortunately, no one was surprised.

Why This Matters

In many workplaces, initiative is everything. Waiting to be guided might leave you behind. Learning to swim, quickly, isn't cruel - it's survival.

No one is going to sit down, hold your hand, and walk you through every detail of your new job. That may sound harsh, but it's the truth, and the sooner you understand it, the better off you'll be.

We live in an age of instant gratification: text me, ping me, answer me now. That same expectation spills into the workplace. Managers are stretched thin. Teams are running lean. Everyone's juggling too much and pretending it's fine. So, when you walk into a new role expecting a carefully laid-out training plan, or a mentor with time to spare, prepare for disappointment.

You were warned back in the *Allow Yourself to Feel Stupid* section. That advice still stands. It's okay to feel lost and confused. What you can't do is use that confusion as an excuse to sit around and wait for someone to save you with a color-coded checklist.

You're Expected to Self-Start

In most workplaces today, your onboarding is more of a drive-by than a deep dive. A manager might toss you a few bullet points in a kickoff meeting, rattle off a vague summary like, *"We usually run that report every Friday,"* and then – poof - they're off to their fifth Zoom call of the morning. No formal training, no comprehensive handbook, and definitely no warm welcome committee walking you through it step by step. Here's the uncomfortable truth: that's normal now.

If you want to survive, you'll need to be your own teacher, coach, cheerleader, and systems architect. Here's how:

1. Ask Clarifying Questions

Yes, even the ones that feel dumb. Ask them anyway. Ask them twice if you have to. This is not the time to let pride or fear make you look "quietly capable" when you're just quietly drowning.

Good clarifying questions include:
- "Can you walk me through that one more time?"
- "What would success look like for this task?"
- "Who else on the team might be able to give me more context?"

2. Shadow Someone When You Can

Even if it's unofficial. Sit in on meetings. Offer to take notes. Ask to watch how they submit a ticket, update a report, or format a client deck. Observation is education. One hour shadowing the right person will teach you more than ten hours staring at confusing emails.

3. Use Your AI Tools (Hello, ChatGPT)

Don't know what "quarterly reconciliation" means? Not sure how to write a professional follow-up email? Tasked with organizing a spreadsheet but Excel looks like the Matrix? Ask. The. Robot. AI isn't here to replace you, it's here to equip you. It won't do the job for you, but it'll help you figure out what you don't yet know.

4. Research. Read. Try. Fail. Try Again.

Treat your job like a puzzle. Look at examples. Google acronyms. Test things. Break things. Watch what happens. Learn from it. If you're not making at least one mistake a week while trying something new, you're not growing.

5. Take Notes Like Your Life Depends On It

DO NOT rely on your memory. By 10:00 a.m., you won't remember what you had for breakfast. Things will be flying at you so fast it'll feel like your brain is buffering in real time. Instead, build a system. Start a living document, digital notebook, or running email draft, whatever works for your brain. The key is consistency.

Write down:
- What worked and what didn't.
- Who to ask for what.
- Where to find files, folders, or past examples.
- Processes, tips, hacks.
- Any weird company lingo no one explained (but everyone seems to know).
- Deadlines, deliverables, and details because they matter more than you think.

This becomes your personal knowledge bank. When your brain is fried and someone hits you with *"Hey, remember what we did last quarter?"* you won't panic. You'll scroll. You'll shine. You'll be ready.

The Time You Want Doesn't Exist—Yet

Let's kill the fantasy right now: you're not going to stroll into a well-organized job and receive an extensive training manual. There will not be a predecessor waiting to walk you through every task like you're on a tour at Disneyland. That's not real life. In most workplaces, the person before you left in a rush. They barely had time to clear their inbox, let alone document anything for you. And your new co-workers? They're likely juggling their own overflowing to-do lists and won't be able to spoon-feed you every detail.

So, what does that mean for you? It means you're going to have to make time to learn it on your own. Not find it - make it. Carve it out. Fight for it. Especially in the beginning.

Here's the not-so-glamorous but necessary truth: You will spend more time learning your job outside the 8–5 hours than during it. Expect to spend more time learning your job outside the office hours than during it. Some nights will run late. Dinner might happen in front of a tutorial video. Reports may need rewriting two, even three times before they're right - long after everyone else has logged off.

That effort? It compounds. The time you put in now builds confidence later. The gaps you close on your own become your competitive edge. Because while some people coast, you're building:

- Mental muscle to think more strategically.
- Emotional muscle to navigate high-pressure moments.
- Professional muscle to become the person people turn to for answers—not away from when problems hit.

Want to coast? Great. Do the bare minimum, clock in and out, and stay exactly where you are. Or do you want to level up? Show up differently. Be hungry. Be humble. Learn proactively.

"But That's Not Fair!"

Nope, it's not. But neither is corporate culture, promotions, or the fact that the woman in accounting has been wearing her crown like it's Squid Game meets The Hunger Games since you arrived. This isn't about being fair; it's about being prepared. Once you accept that no one's coming to rescue you with a how-to manual, you start to see just how capable you really are. You stop waiting and start doing it.

Key Truth: The workplace isn't designed to nurture. It's designed to produce. If you want nurturing, go to therapy. If you want to win at work, get ready to hustle smart and teach yourself fast.

Know Before You Go

Before you clock in for your first job, start building your own knowledge base. The next page provides *a Job Knowledge Starter Checklist*. This checklist isn't homework; it's your head start. You may not know exactly what your role will require yet but getting curious now sets the tone for how you'll show up. The more you prepare on your own, the faster you'll adapt and the less overwhelmed you'll feel when everything starts coming at you fast. Think of this as your personal pre-game plan.

Job Knowledge Starter Checklist

Think of this as your warm-up lap before the real race. Don't wait until your first day to realize you don't know the difference between CRM and KPI. Use this list to get ahead now so you're walking in confident, not frantically Googling acronyms in the bathroom.

1. Industry Buzzwords & Acronyms
Nothing feels worse than sitting in a meeting where everyone's nodding and you're thinking, "What even is ROI?"

Word or Acronym	What It *Actually* Means	Where to Look It Up (Google, company site, ChatGPT, etc.)

2. Rules: Written and Unwritten
Yes, privacy laws, ethics, and compliance matter, but so do the **unspoken rules** (like don't reply-all with "thanks"). Start clocking both.

Topic (e.g., privacy, safety, ethics, "meeting etiquette")	Why It Matters	Where to Start

3. Tools You'll Be Expected to Magically Know
Excel formulas, Slack channels, Canva templates… the things no one will train you on, but everyone assumes you get. A 10-minute YouTube tutorial can save you 10 weeks of embarrassment.

Tool / Platform	Why Everyone Pretends They Already Know How to Use It	Free Ways to Learn

4. Job Roles You'll Cross Paths With

Titles mean less than power dynamics. Know who does what, but also notice: Who slows things down? Who solves things fast? Who gets listened to, and who gets ignored? That's the real org chart.

Role Title	What They *Actually* Do	Notes / Questions You Have

5. What You Wish They'd Teach You

"Figuring It Out" is the unofficial training program. Keep track of what you don't know so you can ask the right people—or find the right hacks—before it derails you.

"I Don't Know…"	Who Might Know	How I'll Find Out

6. Culture Clues & First Impressions

Every workplace has its own unspoken dress code, slang, and vibe. Pay attention: what's celebrated here, and what gets side-eyed?

What I've Heard or Noticed	What That Might Mean	Questions I Have

Bottom line: Nobody's going to hand you a perfect playbook on day one. But with this checklist, you're already writing your own. That's how you go from rookie to resource - fast.

THE INVISIBLE WALL

Warning: this next section might ruffle a few feathers. But if we're serious about decoding workplace culture and calling out the dynamics that shape it, then we can't skip this conversation.

Beyond generational influences, there's another major factor dividing women in the workplace: mothers and non-mothers.

Two groups. One workplace. And a whole lot of assumptions, frustrations, and misunderstandings in between.

Before we dive in, let me say this clearly - this isn't a judgment zone. I'm not here to promote or shame either side. I've been both during my career, and I've seen firsthand the unique challenges and strengths that each perspective brings to the table. What follows is not scientific data. It's observation. It's pattern recognition. It's twenty plus years of watching women interact in real-time professional settings.

And it's time we talked about it.

Two Different Operating Systems

When I say "mothers," I mean women who are currently raising children or have raised them.

When I say "non-mothers," I'm referring to women who have not raised children, whether by choice, circumstance, or season of life.

Both are equally valuable! But the hard truth: they often operate on completely different bandwidths and that difference can lead to real tension if it's not acknowledged.

Mothers in the Workplace

Mothers tend to excel at multitasking, setting boundaries, and managing competing priorities. That's not a stereotype; it's a skillset honed by real life. When you've juggled work emails with daycare pick-up, conference calls with sick kids, and budget meetings with school supply runs, you learn how to pivot fast and get things done under pressure.

Mothers often:
- Work efficiently in bursts.
- Collaborate well (because they don't have time for ego games).
- Prioritize team harmony.
- Know how to redirect chaos into structure.
- Have a higher tolerance for imperfection (because perfection was left back in the diaper bag).

But here's the catch: because their time is limited and heavily scheduled, they may set firmer boundaries. That can sometimes come off as detached or less committed to the job.

Spoiler: it's not about commitment; it's about capacity.

Non-Mothers in the Workplace

Non-mothers often show up with intense focus, unshakeable drive, and a laser-like commitment to their work. Many take on extra responsibilities, longer hours, or leadership roles faster because they can.

Non-mothers often:
- Stay late or log back in after hours.
- Take on complex projects without the same personal scheduling conflicts.
- Dive deep into strategy and execution.
- Move up the ladder quickly.
- Are seen (and sometimes expect to be treated) as the most dependable "go-to" person.

These traits come with their set tensions: Non-mothers are often expected to "pick up the slack" without complaint. They may feel overlooked for time off or resented for having more flexibility in their schedule.

Over time, if no one names these dynamics, quiet resentments start stacking up on both sides.

The Tension No One Talks About

The reality:
- Some non-mothers feel like they're doing double the work while mothers get a "pass."
- Some mothers feel silently judged for not staying late or declining extra meetings.
- Both feel like they can't win.

If you're a mother, you may worry that taking time off for your child's needs makes you look less committed, even when your world is falling apart at home.

If you're not a mother, you may feel you're expected to prove yourself twice as hard just because you don't have a "valid excuse" to say no. And when you *do* take a personal day for your own mental health or rest, the guilt creeps in because it doesn't feel "justified" enough.

Each group is fighting its own invisible battle and they're both carrying guilt that no one sees. Guilt for missing time, or needing time, and for choosing yourself in a world that rewards burnout. The only way to shift the narrative isn't to compare sacrifices, but to acknowledge the weight we're all carrying and stop assuming we know each other's reasons.

Why This Matters

Understanding the unique pressures and strengths of each group isn't just a "nice-to-have," it's the key to working smarter, and more compassionately, together. Because if we keep viewing each other as competition - if we assume one lifestyle is easier, one sacrifice is greater, or one work ethic is stronger - we're just reinforcing the same harmful dynamics we claim we want to change.

As a rising professional, whether you plan to become a parent one day or not, you have the opportunity to break this cycle. You can be the generation that stops the bickering, the side-eyes, and the unspoken resentments. But only if you walk in with awareness, not assumptions.

Recognizing these dynamics early gives you an advantage that took most women years (and therapy) to figure out. Understand this:

- **Mothers** often expect new professionals to be dependable, respectful of time, and self-sufficient. Why? They don't have the capacity to handhold, because they're juggling a lot, and they've earned their efficiency.
- **Non-mothers** may expect you to rise quickly, match their focus, and prove you're committed. Why? They've been expected to overperform and may see their identity tied to their professional output.

Neither is wrong, but both come with their own lens. If you can see it clearly now, you'll work smarter later and you won't take either side's behavior so personally.

Whether you're a mother or not, your presence in the workplace matters. Your value isn't tied to your family status. It's tied to how you show up and how you treat the women around you. That's the kind of legacy we need to promote to change things.

It all Comes Down to Compassion

The more we understand what drives one another - the choices, the sacrifices, the unseen pressure - the more we can start creating workplaces where women support women across every social class. You don't have to share someone's life experience to show them grace. But you do have to learn how to *read the room* and respond with empathy, not ego.

If You're Working with a Mother, she might:
- Come in late one day, juggling daycare drop-off and a toddler meltdown.
- Leave early for a school program.
- Seem distracted; but she's mentally tracking 35 different things, including that email thread you're stressing over.

When she's having a difficult day:
- Don't assume she's uncommitted.
- Offer clarity, not criticism.
- Step in with support, not superiority.

Survival Tip: Be helpful, not nosy. A quick "I've got this if you need to step away for a bit" goes miles further than asking if she's okay for the fifth time.

If You're Working with a Non-Mother, she might:
- Be the last one to leave and the first one to show up.
- Have been overlooked or expected to take on more "because she doesn't have kids."
- Be intense, driven, or guarded, and she might not want to chit-chat about your family.

When she's having a difficult day:
- Don't dismiss her stress just because she doesn't have a "home reason."
- Avoid saying things like "You don't even have kids, how are you so tired?"
- Respect her boundaries and professionalism, don't confuse them for coldness.

Survival Tip: Respect her workload and offer collaboration instead of competition. A simple "Want to divide and conquer this?" can turn tension into teamwork.

What You Can Do:

As a rising professional, you have the power to break the cycle. Whether you plan to become a parent or not, you can model a new way forward: one built on mutual respect, open communication, and zero tolerance for assumptions.

Your generation of professionals is more emotionally aware and socially conscious than ever before. Use that as leverage. Don't just work next to each other, work *with* each other. Because that's how change happens. Not through policy, but through practice.

YOUR SUPERPOWER

A junior employee once told me, *"I thought I was doing something wrong, until I realized it was the system."* That moment? Game-changer. Her entire posture shifted, because once you name the problem, you stop blaming yourself for it.

Why This Matters:

Once you recognize patterns, you reclaim your power. You're no longer just reacting, you're choosing and that's the first survival skill every workplace newcomer needs.

You can have the highest GPA, the most polished résumé, and even the best ideas in the room, but if you don't know how to read people, you're going to struggle. Emotional intelligence (EQ) is the difference between being seen as promising and being dismissed as "not ready."

What does "Reading the Room" really mean?

It's not about being fake or "kissing up." It's about paying attention and slowing down long enough to *observe* before you act. Reading the room means:

- Noticing subtle shifts in energy and tone
- Noticing who's aligned with who and who's constantly on edge.
- Recognizing when your question is curious and when it's poorly timed.
- Adjusting your delivery without losing your voice

What *Is* Emotional Intelligence, Anyway?

Emotional intelligence (EQ) is your ability to recognize, understand, and manage emotions - your own and other people's. It's not about being soft or emotional. It's about being street smart with feelings in high-stakes spaces.

Think of it as four key skills:

1. **Self-awareness:**

   Knowing what you're feeling and why, so your emotions don't run the show without your permission.

2. **Self-regulation:**

   Staying calm under pressure, responding instead of reacting, and choosing your behavior instead of letting it choose you.

3. **Social awareness:**

   Noticing unspoken dynamics, and picking up on tone, body language, and the vibe no one says aloud.

4. **Relationship management:**

   Navigating conflict, building trust, giving feedback, and communicating clearly even when things get messy.

High EQ doesn't mean you're a pushover. It means you know when to pause, when to pivot, and when to *own* the room without blowing it up.

💬 *If knowledge is power, EQ is the translator. It turns what you know into influence that people follow.*

First-Job Stumbles That Kill Credibility

You've got to know when to speak, when to watch, and when to take notes for later. Here are common rookie moves:

Over-eagerness.

Jumping into conversations that aren't yours, volunteering for everything without understanding the power dynamics, or pushing your ideas without learning the history behind a process.

Over-sharing.

Trying to "bond" by disclosing too much too soon, or worse, gossiping to feel included.

Mistaking silence for agreement.

Just because no one speaks up doesn't mean they co-sign your opinion. Sometimes silence is code for: "We're all thinking this is a bad idea."

Overconfidence without awareness.

You may know your stuff, but if you come in acting like you've got it all figured out, you'll lose allies fast. Nobody likes a know-it-all who's never had to earn it.

The Skill That Wins? Observation.

Want to level up fast? Shut up and watch first. Notice:
- Who leads the room.
- Who listens with intention.
- Who gets cut off, and who never does.
- Who influences quietly versus loudly.

Don't just study what people do, study how they do it. That's the hidden playbook.

Assertive ≠ Aggressive

This one's especially important for women in the workplace. You've been told to "speak up," "be bold," or "take initiative." That's not bad advice, but timing and tone matter. There's a difference between:
- "Here's how I can help." vs.
- "Here's what you're doing wrong."

One invites collaboration. The other invites resistance. Own your voice, but don't weaponize it.

Use EQ Like a Strategy

EQ is not just about being nice. It's about being smart with your energy and intentional with your presence. Start with small habits:
- Mirror the energy of a tense meeting instead of trying to lighten the mood too soon.
- If someone seems rushed, ask if it's a suitable time to bring something up.
- Notice cues: eye rolls, foot tapping, flat responses. These are signals.

You can't control their behavior. But you can always control your response. That's the win.

Quick Self-Check:

Ask yourself before you speak up:
- What's the tone of the room right now?
- Has this issue been discussed before? (If so, what happened?)
- Is this the right person to bring this up with—or just the most available one?

Let's Make It Personal

EQ isn't a buzzword. It's one of the most important tools you'll need to survive and thrive in any workplace. The more self-aware you are, the less likely you'll be to react out of fear, frustration, or insecurity and the more powerful your presence becomes.

Before you turn the page, take a few minutes to check in on your own emotional intelligence. The worksheet ahead will help you spot strengths, call out blind spots, and build the muscle memory you'll need for the long game.

EQ Starter Pack: Your Secret Weapon at Work

Forget IQ flexing. In most offices, emotional intelligence (EQ) is the difference between thriving and barely surviving. This worksheet isn't therapy, it's your crash course in reading the room, owning your reactions, and not letting other people's drama drag you down.

1. Self-Awareness: Know Your Triggers Before They Own You

Your emotions will sneak into your emails, your tone, and your face if you don't call them out. Name them first, so they don't run the show.

☐ I can tell when I'm reacting out of fear, ego, or insecurity (not facts).

☐ I notice when my face is saying what my mouth is trying not to.

☐ I'm aware of how my energy shifts a room (for better or worse).

Last week check-in: Write one moment where your emotions drove the bus.
Example: "I snapped in Slack because I thought my boss was ignoring me. Turns out she was in a three-hour budget meeting."

_____
_____
_____

2. Self-Regulation: Don't Let Your Impulses Wreck You

Feel like firing off that email? Slamming the door? Don't. EQ means having a game plan for your hot buttons.

☐ I can pause before I say something I'll regret.

☐ I've got at least one go-to reset strategy (walk, playlist, vent-to-friend).

☐ I can disagree without torching the relationship.

Your strategy list: What 2 things will you do next time you're triggered?
1._____
2._____

3. Social Awareness: Read the Room Like It's a Script

It's not enough to "listen." You've got to clock the dynamics nobody says aloud.

☐ I notice when the vibe shifts, even if no one names it.

☐ I remember that background + experience = different reactions.

☐ I can spot when someone's being sidelined, dismissed, or straight-up ignored.

Confession time: Describe a moment you totally misread the vibe. What did it teach you?

_____
_____
_____

4. Relationship Management: Handle People Without Losing Yourself

Work is basically group projects forever. The goal? Stay real, stay clear, and build trust you can cash in later.

☐ I can take feedback without spiraling.

☐ I know how to fix trust when I break it.

☐ I can speak up in tense moments without blowing things up.

Pick one area you'll level up in the next 90 days

_____
_____
_____

Your EQ Power Move

What's one shift you'll make now to flex your EQ muscle? Write it like a promise. *Example: "I will pause before reacting, so I don't let someone else's chaos become my reputation."*

"I will _____."

💬 *EQ isn't about being nice. It's about being effective. The higher your EQ, the harder it is for someone else's nonsense to derail you. That's power.*

NEON CELL PHONE

Once, during a job interview, a candidate's Instagram popped up on the hiring manager's screen. Beach pics, shots with red solo cups, and a caption that said, "F**k Mondays." Spoiler: she didn't get the job.

Why This Matters:

Like it or not, your digital life bleeds into your professional one. Employers check. Colleagues judge. And reputations are built faster than you can delete a post. Your phone isn't private; it's a billboard with your name splashed across it.

What They See Is Not What You Think You're Doing.

Let's revisit the two top-tier generations we talked about earlier, Baby Boomers and Gen X. Here's something we didn't cover but absolutely need to: they *cannot stand* seeing you on your phone at work. It doesn't matter what you're doing. To them, a phone in your hand means one of two things:

1. You don't have enough work to do;
2. Or you don't care about your job.

That may feel harsh, especially if you *are* working while listening to a business podcast, texting a vendor, managing your calendar, or even drafting notes in your favorite AI app. But remember our chapter on perception? What someone sees is their reality. And for many women in older generations, a phone = distraction = disrespect.

A Common Complaint

I can't tell you how many times I've had a female manager come into my office, arms crossed, tone tight, venting about a younger employee who "just stares at their phone all day." The assumption? Disengaged. Careless. Wasting time.

Here's the twist: when I dug deeper, looked at their output, reviewed their project status, even pulled peer feedback, many of these same employees were not only meeting expectations, but they were also exceeding them. They were fast, efficient, and often outpaced their peers.

So, what's the issue? Their work might be exceptional, but their habits don't look like what older generations recognize as "professional." To a Boomer or Gen X leader, "doing your job" doesn't just mean hitting deadlines, it means appearing focused and present. A phone out, even for work, sends the message: "I'm not fully here."

Once that seed of doubt is planted, it's hard to pull. Trust erodes. Opportunities shrink. Promotions slip by. Not because of results, but because of optics. One manager even told me, *"It doesn't matter if she's doing a great job, I shouldn't have to wonder if she is."*

You can be a high performer and still stall your career if someone thinks you're distracted.

Understand the Backstory

You've grown up in a tech-saturated world. You're used to multitasking between tabs, playlists, and apps. You might even *think better* when music is playing or when switching between devices. But older generations weren't wired this way. They were taught that work looks like this:

- Eyes on screen.
- Hands on keyboard.
- Mouth shut.
- Phone away.

Think Before You Tap

Your phone isn't just a device, it's a spotlight. In a workplace shaped by generations who associate phones with distraction, laziness, and disengagement, every swipe you make can be misunderstood. Here's how to protect your professional reputation without losing your individuality:

- **Use headphones** if you're listening to music or a podcast and keep the volume low. You might focus better with background noise, but others might assume you're zoning out. Earbuds help you concentrate *and* show you're trying to be respectful.

- ☐ **Set your phone face-down or out of sight** when in meetings or shared spaces. Even if you're just checking work messages or using a timer, others will see a glowing screen and assume the worst. Out of sight = fewer assumptions.
- ☐ **Narrate your purpose when necessary.** If you pull out your phone in front of a manager or co-worker, say it aloud:

    "Just pulling up the project timeline," or

    "I'm checking my calendar for the client call."

    A single sentence can prevent hours of gossip and suspicion.
- ☐ **Keep personal scrolling to actual breaks—or private places.** You're allowed to decompress but be smart about where and when. Sitting in the middle of an open office giggling at memes might feel harmless, but it leaves an impression.

Remember:

Your phone habits aren't about what you're doing. They're about how others perceive what you're doing.

Fair? No. Real? Yes.

Protect your image. Guard your focus. And never let a glowing screen become the reason someone doubts your value.

CLOTHES TALK

How Did We Even Get Here?

Once upon a time, corporate America was starched collars, pantyhose, and power suits. Every morning looked like a scene from *Mad Men*, minus the smoking in the breakroom. For decades, dressing for the office meant buttoned-up conformity and a strict separation between "personal" and "professional" style.

But then... tech happened.

Startups ditched the suits for hoodies. Silicon Valley normalized sneakers in boardrooms. Millennials and Gen Z said, *"If I'm getting my work done, why should it matter what I'm wearing?"*

Now we're living in the *business casual era*, where expectations are vague, policies are outdated, and the line between "appropriate" and "offensive" is blurrier than ever.

What Even *Is* Business Casual?

Let's break it down:

Business Casual means professional, but not stiff. It's the middle ground between a full suit and your weekend errand outfit. Think:

- Clean, wrinkle-free pants or skirts
- Collared shirts, blouses, or tailored tops
- Closed-toed shoes or professional flats.
- Cardigans, structured jackets, or blazers (optional but always elevating)

NOT Business Casual:

- Crop tops, spaghetti straps, or sheer anything.
- Ripped jeans or shorts (even "designer" ones)
- Leggings as pants (unless you're in a creative field that openly allows them)
- Slides, flip-flops, or fuzzy slippers—yes, even the designer ones
- Outfits that scream club, brunch, or gym

Pro tip: If you're unsure, dress one level above what you *think* the job calls for, especially when you're new.

Why It Still Matters

You might be thinking, *"I should be judged by my work, not my outfit."* And you're right… in theory. But in practice? The way you show up tells people how seriously you take your role. It communicates effort, respect, and professionalism before you ever open your mouth. And in today's hyper-connected world, your audience isn't just the person sitting next to you.

With modern workplace tools, like Zoom, Teams, LinkedIn, email, your image travels. You could be on a video call with a client in Dubai one minute and then presenting to a board in New York the next. That graphic tee or borderline outfit choice? It may land differently across cultures. What feels casual to you could be perceived as offensive or careless by someone halfway across the globe.

Start thinking globally, not just locally. Your wardrobe isn't just for the office; it's for the world stage your career is on.

Remember what we said about perception becoming reality? Your outfit is part of the unspoken résumé you bring into the room every day. So, make sure it reflects the future you're working toward.

But What About Personal Style?

Let's be clear: no one's asking you to become a corporate clone. You don't have to drain the personality out of your wardrobe to be taken seriously at work. Personal style matters. It's how you show up. It's how you express who you are without saying a word. But here's the secret: the best professional style doesn't erase your personality, it *elevates* it.

This has nothing to do with your culture, your sexual orientation, or your income level. You don't need designer labels, luxury brands, or a Pinterest-perfect closet. You just need intentionality.

Intentionality means doing something *on purpose*, with *clear thought and purpose behind your choices*, rather than just reacting or going with the flow. In the context of dressing for work, intentionality means choosing your outfit with awareness of:

- The environment you're in
- The message you want to send.
- The impression you want to make.

It's the difference between throwing something on because it's clean versus wearing something because it communicates, "I take this seriously."

Proper, professional outfits are accessible to everyone, no matter your budget or background. You can thrift it, borrow it, and build it piece by piece. And you can also be bold, expressive, and still office ready. So yes:

- ✓ Add your color.
- ✓ Rock that pattern.
- ✓ Reflect your unique vibe.

But your outfit shouldn't speak louder than your contributions.

Real Talk Style Mistakes……That People *Will* Talk About:
- Wearing clothes that are too tight, too short, or too low-cut.
- Showing up with wrinkled or dirty clothing (people notice).
- Wearing pajamas or loungewear in a hybrid/remote role on Zoom calls.
- Overdoing perfume or cologne (some folks are allergic - yes, it's a thing.
- Wearing flashy brands that scream more ego than effort.
- Not wearing proper undergarments, or none at all.

Let's just be honest, most men in the workplace aren't paying attention to your outfit details. But other women? They are. Women notice when another woman walks in with wrinkled clothes, visible undergarments, or no bra at all. They may not say it to your face, but they're talking behind your back, and not in a flattering way. A professional environment is not the place to protest fashion norms with exposed cleavage, sheer fabrics, or bouncing body parts. If you want to be taken seriously, start by dressing like you take yourself seriously. That means proper undergarments, well-fitted clothing, and a clear sense of polish. You can still be bold and stylish, but don't let your outfit become the distraction that undermines your credibility.

When your outfit becomes the topic of whispered conversations, you've just handed them a distraction, and another reason to question your judgment. Not because you're not capable, but because you let your wardrobe do the talking *before your work ever gets the chance.*

In short: don't give people a reason to make you a story. Let your professionalism speak for itself, loud, clear, and stylishly on-point.

Still Unsure What Counts as Business Casual?

You're not alone. With so many interpretations floating around, it can feel confusing to know where the line is. The good news? You don't have to guess. On the next page, I've laid it out for you: side-by-side examples of what's considered proper business casual versus what might send the wrong message. Use this as a visual guide to help you make confident, intentional wardrobe choices.

When Your Outfit Talks Louder Than Your Work

Remember: If your outfit becomes the story, your credibility becomes the casualty.

Business Casual: *"Polished, clean, and versatile. Your clothes say, 'I take this seriously.'"*

Inappropriate: *"Wrinkled, sloppy, or club ready. Your outfit overshadows your credibility."*

Note: Business casual may look different across cultures. The key is intentionality - clean, polished, and proper for your setting.

YOU CAN'T UNPOST YOUR REPUTATION

Your posts may disappear from your feed, but not from someone's memory.

Every photo, caption, sarcastic comment, vague post, or cringey TikTok dance all becomes part of your brand. Whether you like it or not, you're building a résumé with your social media. Everything you post online is a breadcrumb, a trail, or a story, and it's one that *everyone* is reading, even the people who say they aren't watching.

You might think your social media is private, or that it's "just for fun," or that what you do on your personal time has no impact on your professional life, but I'm here to tell you that's a dangerous assumption.

I promise you, your co-workers, boss, and even the quiet lady in accounting have scoped out your social profiles. It's human nature, people are curious, especially about new hires. And if you think they aren't screen-grabbing your weekend antics and passing it around in group chats or judgmental breakroom whispers, think again.

Perception is reality, remember? You may have all your tasks done and you may be the hardest worker in the department, but if your social media screams chaos, recklessness, drama, or poor judgement, you're putting a ceiling on your credibility.

The Screenshots Come First - The Consequences Come Later

I've been in HR for over twenty years and let me give you the uncomfortable truth: not only are people watching and judging, but some are also quietly plotting. I've had employees come into my office in tears, blindsided after being passed over for a promotion or even let go, and deep down, they never realized that part of the reason was *what someone pulled up on their phone.*

I've seen:
- Group chats that included screenshots of bikini-clad vacation posts with mocking emojis.

- DMs sending angry political rants captioned, "Is this really someone we want representing the company?"
- Team leaders point out public complaints from employees' personal Facebook pages as reasons to skip them for team lead roles.
- Derogatory comments towards other cultures and races by the sweet and friendly receptionist at the front desk.

It wasn't always fair, but it was always *influential*.

You Are a Brand

In today's world, your social media is your first interview. Your highlight reel is how people get to know you before you ever speak. So, if your profile is full of:
- "Hot mess" captions.
- Cryptic quotes that throw shade at exes or co-workers.
- Half-dressed selfies; or
- Complaints about your job or your boss.

Then don't be surprised when someone starts whispering that you might not be "management material."

Your online presence doesn't just follow you; it speaks for you. Even if your profile is technically "private," and you don't add co-workers, someone can and will find it.

Don't Be the Reason Someone Says, "Not Her'

Employers don't just hire people, they hire risk. If your feed looks reckless, immature, or volatile, you've already made yourself a risk they might not want to take. Even if you're a brilliant worker and the most efficient person on the team, what they see is:
- "Will this person embarrass us at a conference?"
- "Will they post something problematic and spark backlash?"
- "Can we trust them with clients or leadership roles?"

Fair or not, this is how decisions are made in boardrooms and behind closed doors.

I can tell you the utmost certainty, HR and your future boss are absolutely checking your digital footprint. And while no one puts this in the job posting, here's the unspoken truth: your social content might be the deciding factor. If your feed is full of angry rants, bikini selfies captioned "hot mess express," or TikToks of you roasting your last employer, you're getting ghosted after the interview, even if everything else about you is perfect on paper.

If I'm being brutally honest: sometimes women may use your social media content as a reason to hold you back. Don't give them free ammunition. If you're the person posting drunken party pics on Saturday night and asking for a promotion on Monday morning, your co-workers will remember the Saturday, not the spreadsheet. While you're busy thinking, "It's not a big deal," someone else is quietly asking, "Does she really get what this role requires?"

Your Future Self Is Counting on You

Ask any Gen X woman in leadership today and you'll hear a common, honest refrain: "Thank God there were no cell phones when we were younger." We made our mistakes in the moment - at parties, in dorm rooms, on questionable spring break trips - but those moments disappeared when the night ended. There were no videos. No digital footprints. No permanent record living on the Internet, waiting to be unearthed at the worst possible time. You don't get that luxury.

Today, everything is documented. Shared. Reposted. Archived. You're living in a world where every moment has the potential to become part of your long-term reputation, even if it was just a passing post, a joke, or a difficult day.

So, while you might be focused on landing your *first* job right now, you also need to be protecting the version of you who's going to want a *bigger* job later. Because five years from now, when you're interviewing for a leadership role, being considered for a public-facing position, or hoping to represent your company on a panel, a podcast, or a national stage, someone will Google you and pull up your old posts and will ask themselves, "Is this really the image we want associated with our organization?" That's the harsh truth.

Even when you outgrow that version of yourself, the Internet never will. You can't:

- Go back and erase what you shared in a moment of immaturity.
- Hit "unsend" on a tweet that went sideways.
- Explain yourself to someone who only sees the screenshot, and not the growth.

But what you *can* do is start curating your digital footprint now. You can be intentional and strategic and start protecting the professional you're becoming. Because your future self? She's counting on you to make sure nothing dumb you posted at 22 stands between her and the career she's worked hard for at 32.

The Double Life Strategy

No one is telling you to delete your personality. You're allowed to have fun, to celebrate and live. But you must be strategic about how you show it. If you're someone who enjoys posting bold opinions, party photos, dance videos, or spicy takes, do what you need to do - but do it with separation and intentionality.

Here's how to protect yourself:

1. Create a Private Account With Boundaries
- Use a different version of your name, something not easily searchable.
- Lock it down tight - private settings, limited followers, no tagging co-workers.

- Skip the bio that links to your real job or your full name. This is not your networking space.

2. Don't Mix Work and Play
- Do not link this account to your LinkedIn profile.
- Don't follow your boss, co-workers, clients, or recruiters.
- Avoid tagging your workplace in posts or bios - this is how personal content ends up in professional circles.

3. Curate Your Public Presence

For your public-facing profiles (Instagram, TikTok, even Facebook if you keep it active), assume every post could be:
- Screenshot and sent to a hiring manager.
- Used in a conversation you're not part of.
- Evaluated in a professional setting, fairly or not.

1. Use your professional space to showcase:
- Your passions in a professional light.
- Volunteer work, career milestones, hobbies, or skill-building efforts.
- Posts that align with your values, ambitions, and long-term goals.

The solution isn't to hide who you are; it's to be *smart* about what version of yourself you're sharing, and where you share it. Your brand doesn't start when you walk into the office, it starts the moment someone Googles your name.

Audit Before You Post

Before you hit post, ask yourself:
- Would I want this shown in a team meeting?
- Would I want a future boss to see this?
- Would I want this to define me when I'm not in the room?

If the answer's no, then do yourself a favor and keep it off the feed.

Your digital footprint is part of your professional identity whether you realize it or not. Every photo, comment, or story reflects how seriously you take yourself and your future. That's why a regular self-audit is crucial. Not to censor who you are, but to *protect who you're becoming.*

Take a few minutes to complete the *Social Media Self Audit Worksheet* that follows. It's your chance to look at your online presence with fresh eyes: the way a recruiter, manager, or future collaborator might. If there's anything that doesn't align with the reputation you're building, now's the time to clean it up. Your career is already speaking, make sure it's saying the right things.

Social Media Self-Audit Worksheet

Your Reputation Is Just a Click Away: What you post is a headline for who you are. Make sure it's one you're proud of.

Step 1: Inventory Your Digital Footprint
List your current social media accounts (public and private):

Platform	Handle/Name Used	Private or Public?	Connected to Work (Y/N)?
Instagram			
Facebook			
TikTok			
Twitter/X			
Snapchat			
LinkedIn			
Other:			

Step 2: Scroll Through Like a Stranger
Go through your public profiles and answer the following:

1. Do your posts reflect your professional goals or values?
   ☐ Yes ☐ No

2. Would you be comfortable with your manager or future employer seeing your latest 10 posts/stories?
   ☐ Yes ☐ No

3. Are you tagged in any photos or comments that could raise questions about your judgment?
   ☐ Yes ☐ No

4. Do you post content that could be seen as disrespectful, offensive, or polarizing?
   ☐ Yes ☐ No

5. Do you maintain clear boundaries between your personal and professional content?
   ☐ Yes ☐ No

Step 3: Clean Up the Digital Clutter
For any red flags you identified, list what actions you'll take:

Content Concern (Post/Tag/Comment)	Platform	Action Needed (Delete, Un-tag, Archive)	Deadline

Step 4: Build a Stronger Public Image
Reflect and answer:

- What *three words* do I want my social media to communicate about me?
   1. _____
   2. _____
   3. _____

- What kind of content could I post that supports those three words?

Final Check: The Screenshot Rule

Before you post anything new, ask yourself:

Would I be okay with this being screenshot, emailed to my boss, and brought up in a job interview?
☐ Yes
☐ No → Then don't post it.

LOVE & PAYCHECKS DON'T MIX

Let's not sugarcoat it: dating a co-worker might seem thrilling, but it opens the door to a professional minefield you're not prepared to handle. Depending on the size of the organization, you may not even realize you're competing for someone's attention until you're suddenly a target. Workplace crushes come with silent spectators, and when personal lives mix with professional ones, jealousy, gossip, and sabotage are never far behind. If you happen to end up dating the person they had their eye on? Buckle up. You've just bought a one-way ticket to drama and sabotage.

Even if your relationship feels mature and healthy, the perception of favoritism will follow you like a shadow, especially if your partner is in leadership. You might be the most qualified, hardest-working woman on the team, but once you're in a relationship with a co-worker, your achievements get tainted by whispers: *"Oh, she only got that role because of who she's dating."* And those whispers? They can ruin your credibility faster than a bad performance review. Perception spreads faster than facts, and once people think you're climbing through romance instead of results, you'll never control the story again.

If you find yourself in a worksite romance, you don't have endless options. Realistically, you face three paths:
1. Find another job.
2. Break up with that person.
3. Stay silent, brace yourself, and hope the fallout doesn't derail your career.

None of these path's lead to happily-ever-after in the office. They all cost you something: your love life, your job, or your peace.

Let's talk about breakups, because it's not *if,* it's *when*. Relationships end. When that happens, you'll still have to walk into work, sit through meetings, and act like everything's fine while others gossip behind your back. You're not just risking your heart, you're risking your reputation, your paycheck, and your trajectory.

Married Co-Workers Aren't Flirting. They're Testing.

If a married co-worker starts flirting with you, understand this, it's:

- Cute? No.
- Flattering? Never.
- A trap? Every single time.

That co-worker is not going to leave their spouse. The minute you engage, the power dynamic shifts, and not in your favor. You'll be labeled, shamed, and isolated, even if *they* were the one who started it. Why? Because in most workplaces, people are far quicker to judge the woman than the partner who broke their vows.

If you think this doesn't happen in your industry, you're wrong. It happens everywhere, and it's one of the oldest workplace games. New hires are especially vulnerable because they haven't yet learned the warning signs.

Spotting the Warning Signs Before It's Too Late

Workplace flirtation rarely shows up as a neon sign; it creeps in quietly, disguised as jokes, "friendly" gestures, or attention that feels flattering at first. If you don't spot the red flags early, you can find yourself tangled in a situation that threatens your reputation before you even realize what happened. Here are the signs to watch for:

Warning Signs of a Workplace Trap:

- **Private compliments that feel a little too personal** ("You look better than anyone else in this office today").
- **"Accidental" touches or lingering proximity** that cross professional boundaries.
- **Excessive direct messages or late-night texts** that have nothing to do with work.
- **Inside jokes or whispered side conversations** meant to create exclusivity with you.
- **Testing your reaction with offhand comments** about attraction, relationships, or their marriage/partner.
- **Sudden offers of special favors or help** that come with an unspoken expectation.
- **Invitations to "just grab a drink" alone** that somehow don't include anyone else from the team.

Flattery, secrecy, and blurred boundaries aren't signs of connection, they're red flags. If you notice these patterns, don't rationalize them away. Protect your name, your focus, and your future by setting firm boundaries early. In the workplace, prevention is protection, and recognizing the signs before they spiral is the smartest career move you can make.

Real-World Fallout: When Office Romance Becomes Scandal

You don't have to look far to see how damaging workplace romance can be. Just scroll the headlines. Not long ago, a Fortune 500 CEO lost his career overnight when his relationship with an employee went public. The narrative wasn't about the years of leadership he had under his belt. It was about one decision that blurred the lines. Overnight, he went from "visionary leader" to "cautionary tale." And the woman involved? She was reduced to whispers, labeled as opportunistic, even if she had real talent and ambition of her own.

In another case, a well-loved public figure in the music world faced a firestorm after reports of an inappropriate workplace relationship surfaced. The scandal didn't just end a relationship, it ended careers, cost millions in reputation damage, and reminded the world how quickly private choices become public consequences.

Here's the truth: nobody remembers the profits or the projects. They remember the scandal, the screenshots, the whispers, and you don't want your name in that story.

Protect the Career You're Building

Remember what we discussed earlier about insecurities? This is where they will also show up. If you're not secure in your value, you'll confuse validation with affection and fall for behavior you'd never tolerate if you were grounded in your self-worth.

You worked hard to get here. Don't throw away your credibility for a connection that could compromise everything you're building.

This isn't about judging who you date, it's about recognizing that *where* you date changes how you're perceived, and perception matters more than you think. Romance at work comes with invisible strings, and once those strings get pulled - by jealousy, gossip, favoritism, or heartbreak - it's almost impossible to untangle them without damage.

You owe it to yourself, and your future self, to set boundaries now, not when it's already too late. The smartest career move you'll ever make might just be the relationship you never started.

Workplace Relationships: Boundaries & Blind Spots Worksheet

The easiest way to avoid career chaos? **Set your boundaries before someone tests them.** Don't wait until you're in the moment, decide now. Be honest. Your career (and sanity) may depend on it.

1. What boundaries will I set about workplace relationships?
- ☐ I will not date anyone I work directly with
- ☐ I will not date someone with authority over my role
- ☐ I will not date anyone at work at all
- ☐ I will keep all personal relationships strictly outside of work hours and spaces
- ☐ I will discuss and disclose relationships to HR if policy requires

Other boundaries I want to set:
_____
_____
_____
_____

2. What risks do I acknowledge if I choose to date a co-worker?
- ☐ Damaged reputation
- ☐ Favoritism accusations
- ☐ Gossip and sabotage
- ☐ Career progression being questioned
- ☐ Complications if the relationship ends

Dating at work isn't just romance, its reputation roulette.

How would I manage or respond to these risks?
_____
_____
_____
_____

3. How will I handle inappropriate advances at work (especially from married or senior employees)?
- ☐ Have a firm, polite "shut it down" phrase prepared
- ☐ Report the behavior to HR or a trusted leader
- ☐ Remove myself from situations that make me uncomfortable
- ☐ Avoid interpreting attention as validation

Sample phrase I could use to shut it down:

_____

(e.g., "Let's keep this professional." / "That's not appropriate.")

4. What red flags will I not ignore?
- ☐ Flirting from someone in a leadership position
- ☐ Colleagues gossiping about other workplace relationships
- ☐ Someone love-bombing me early in the relationship
- ☐ "Justification" that their marriage is over
- ☐ Requests to keep things secret
- ☐ Work DMs that suddenly shift from tasks to personal compliments

If I see these red flags, I will:

_____
_____
_____
_____

5. What support system can I turn to outside of work if I need advice?
(Write names or roles of people you trust to give you honest, grounded advice.)

_____
_____
_____
_____

Bottom Line:

Write one sentence that summarizes your personal stance on mixing business with pleasure:

_____

This is your non-negotiable. When temptation shows up, this is the line you don't cross.

THIS IS NOT HIS FIGHT

A young employee once asked why her male manager didn't intervene when a female co-worker repeatedly excluded her from meetings. The response? "He doesn't want to get caught in what he dismisses as 'drama between women.'"

Why This Matters

Waiting for male allies won't save you. Learn to advocate for yourself and support other women in doing the same. Culture shifts when we stop outsourcing accountability.

Ask any man about women in the workplace and watch what happens. First, a polite chuckle. Then, a hard pivot to any other subject. Why? Because most men don't want to get involved. They've seen how ruthless women can be with each other, how alliances turn into silent wars, how praise turns into sabotage, and how a side-eye in a meeting can say more than a full performance review. Rather than step in, many men would rather stay out of it completely - especially if he's your boss.

If you go to a male manager seeking help with another woman, don't be surprised when you get a brush-off. You'll hear things like:

- "Just talk to her directly."
- "I'm sure it's just a misunderstanding."
- "You should probably bring this to HR."

Translation? He doesn't want to touch it. Not because he doesn't care, but because he's seen the fallout that happens when men try to mediate drama between women. If he sides with you, he risks being accused of favoritism. If he sides with her, he risks being labeled sexist. And if he tries to stay neutral, everyone ends up frustrated. So, he does what most men do: avoids the mess altogether.

Here's the kicker: even if you have a male mentor, a supportive male colleague, or a guy on the team who genuinely has your back, don't expect him to solve interpersonal conflicts for you.

That's not what allies are for.

You don't need someone to swoop in and "fix" things for you. You need to become the kind of woman who knows how to navigate complexity without waiting for a rescue. While men might be your peers, managers, or even champions… they will not be your shield. They will nod. They may sympathize. They may even agree with your concerns privately. But they won't get in the mud with you. They won't risk their own position to referee your emotional tug-of-war with another woman. And they won't undo the harm caused by another woman's insecurity, jealousy, or quiet sabotage.

Real Talk Example

At one of my former jobs, a new hire, we'll call her Brittany, joined the accounting department with big energy, lofty ideas, and an impressive résumé. From day one, it was clear she had talent. What she didn't have? A heads-up about the two senior women on her team who viewed any new woman as a threat.

They didn't overtly sabotage her. Instead, they iced her out of meetings. Dismissed her ideas in front of leadership, then pitched those same ideas later as their own. They shared "feedback" with her male manager, painting her as inexperienced and arrogant.

Brittany, feeling confused and overwhelmed, finally went to her boss for help. He listened politely and nodded. But his response? "Sounds like a misunderstanding. Maybe just take them out for coffee and talk it through." That was it. No follow-up. No accountability. No effort to get involved.

Brittany did take one of them out for coffee and got a 30-minute monologue about how "young women these days don't know how to be team players."

Eventually, Brittany left the company. Not because she wasn't qualified, or because she couldn't do the job; she left because the environment was harmful and the men in leadership chose to stay neutral.

Real-World Fallout: Silence and Sabotage in Action

You don't have to look far to see what happens when workplace relationships spiral without accountability. Just scroll the headlines:

Uber's "Queen Bee" Culture

When Uber's toxic culture was exposed in 2017, much of the spotlight was on sexual harassment and leadership failure. But buried in the details was another dynamic: women undermining other women. Female managers, instead of mentoring, often acted as gatekeepers, protecting their turf by dismissing or sidelining other women. Meanwhile, male leaders looked the other way, writing it off as "just personality clashes." The result? A culture where women weren't just battling sexism, they were battling each other, while the men in charge stayed neutral.

Ellen Pao vs. Kleiner Perkins

In 2012, Ellen Pao sued one of Silicon Valley's most prestigious venture capital firms for gender discrimination. What made headlines wasn't just her claims of exclusion and retaliation, but how the male partners responded: they didn't intervene. They distanced themselves. Instead of addressing the culture, they preserved it. Pao lost the case, but her story forced a national conversation about bias and the cost of male silence. Once again, the message was clear: waiting for men to step in is a losing strategy.

Whether its women turning on each other or men choosing not to get involved, the result is the same: silence protects the status quo. That's why awareness, boundaries, and self-advocacy matter, because no one else is coming to untangle the mess for you.

So What Do You Do?

You can't control other people's behavior, but you can control how you show up. Here's your playbook:

1. **Lead with clarity, not drama:** That means sticking to facts, not feelings. Instead of saying, "She's always trying to exclude me," say, "I was left off two meetings this week that directly impact my project deliverables." Facts invite solutions. Drama invites defensiveness.

2. **Set boundaries early and reinforce them often:** If someone tries to pull you into gossip, shut it down with a neutral line like, *"I'd rather stay focused on the project."* Boundaries aren't one-time announcements; they're repeated actions that teach people how to treat you.

3. **Document interactions and protect your reputation**: Save emails. Take notes after tense conversations. Keep a running record of decisions, agreements, and moments where you were excluded or undermined. Documentation isn't petty - it's protection. When things escalate, it's your receipts that will speak.

4. **Use emotional intelligence to respond, not react**: Pause before firing off that defensive email. Read the room before you jump in. Ask yourself: *"What outcome do I want here?"* Respond in a way that moves you closer to that goal, instead of just venting your frustration.

5. **Bring it to HR with professionalism, not emotion**: If the line is crossed, don't storm in with "She's out to get me." Instead, present clear, documented patterns: *"Over the past month, I've been excluded from four meetings, and my deliverables were reassigned without explanation. Here are the dates and emails."* HR takes you seriously when you present data, not drama.

Own the Truth, Then Own the Room

Men aren't avoiding your workplace challenges out of malice; they're avoiding them out of self-preservation. Most don't fully understand the layers of tension between women, and they don't want to risk getting dragged into something they can't fix and might get blamed for. So don't waste energy waiting for someone else to step in. Learn to be your own advocate.

It doesn't mean you go at it alone. It means you get smart: you document, communicate with clarity, and know the difference between gossip and strategy. Once you stop expecting a rescue, you start showing up with power. And that's when things start to shift, not just for you, but for every woman watching.

THE BREAKROOM IS NOT A THERAPY ROOM

A junior analyst once cried to me because she found out her desk mate had shared details from a private conversation, one that started with "please don't tell anyone." Spoiler: Everyone knew by Friday.

Why This Matters:

Vulnerability is powerful, but boundaries are necessary. Oversharing at work can blur lines, backfire, and damage trust. Choose wisely where you process your pain; there's a fine line between building rapport and building a case against yourself.

Just like we talked about in the chapter on social media, you need to protect your narrative. That includes what you say out loud at work. Meaning: stop treating your workplace like your therapist's office. Do not start unloading your family drama, friendship fights, or relationship breakdowns in the break room. Why? Because just like your online posts, that personal information becomes a weapon in the wrong hands.

Let me make it plain: you may think you're confiding in a friend, but you're arming a co-worker with gossip fuel. The office is not your safe space. It's your professional stage. Every interaction adds to the story people tell themselves about you. Are you the steady, dependable one who can lead a project under pressure? Or the one who always seems to have a crisis bubbling just under the surface?

You might be crushing deadlines and be the most technically capable person on the team, but if the emotional energy you bring into meetings, casual conversations, or team check-ins is consistently scattered, or frazzled, people will quietly start to associate that with your competence. This is how reputations form: not in big, dramatic moments, but in the subtle patterns people notice and remember. When the time comes for a promotion, a big project, or an annual review, you'll be stunned to learn that what you shared in private was whispered around in judgment.

A Real Talk Example

Sarah was one of the kindest employees you'd ever meet. Generous with her time. Friendly with everyone. But her personal life? A mess.

Her sister had lost custody of her kids, and they were suddenly placed with Sarah. The situation was heartbreaking and heavy. Instead of managing boundaries, Sarah bled her story into the workplace. Every day brought added details about her sister's addiction, court battles, and the strain on Sarah's home. While her co-workers smiled politely and offered sympathy, they were also quietly tallying her drama.

When Sarah sat down for her annual review, she was crushed. Feedback from her female peers painted a vastly different picture than the support she thought she had. Words like "distracted," "overwhelmed," and "unreliable" filled the page. From the same women who had once sat beside her, nodding in sympathy.

What You Share Will Be Used

This isn't a call to become cold, robotic, or fake at work. It's a wake-up call. While you may be performing well in your tasks, what people remember is the energy you bring into the room. If your energy is consistently chaotic or heavy, people will associate that with your competence, even if it's not fair.

You wouldn't show up to a board meeting with a megaphone shouting, "My life is falling apart!" But when you use the break room, Teams chat, or lunch table to vent constantly about your harmful friend group, your boyfriend's betrayal, or your family drama, you've handed people the emotional equivalent of a megaphone. Same impact. Different volume.

Let's be blunt:
- Your co-workers aren't your sisters.
- Your boss isn't your counselor.
- And your cubicle neighbor isn't your journal.

No one is going to stop you from oversharing; but they will start watching you differently because of it. They'll store that information, not for your benefit, but for their strategic use later. Because in a competitive environment, every perceived weakness becomes a potential advantage for someone else.

The HR Reality Check

In all my years in HR, I saw the same pattern play out over and over: the employees who couldn't separate their personal chaos from their professional responsibilities were always the ones sitting in corrective action meetings. Not because they weren't smart or capable, but because their energy was so tied up in drama that their work slipped. If you don't learn how to draw that line, it won't matter who signs your paycheck - different company, different boss, different title - you'll still run into the same problems. Until you get serious about boundaries, your career will always feel like it's one crisis away from collapse.

If your inability to separate work and personal life starts showing up in HR files, it will have a ripple effect on how every colleague and leader perceives you.

The Hidden Consequences of Oversharing

Oversharing doesn't just make things awkward, it creates ripple effects you may not even realize until it's too late.

- **Lost Opportunities** – Leadership may quietly pass you over for a high-profile project because they "aren't sure you can handle the stress."
- **Damaged Credibility** – Even when your work is excellent, colleagues may doubt your professionalism if your personal drama is always front and center.
- **Shifted Perceptions** – Instead of being seen as capable, you risk being labeled "the emotional one," and that reputation sticks.
- **Broken Trust** – If coworkers feel you can't separate personal from professional, they'll be less likely to confide in you- or include you- in key projects.
- **Office Politics Ammo** – Every detail you share is potential gossip fodder, and in competitive environments, someone *will* use it against you.
- **Energy Drain** – Reliving your problems at work keeps you stuck in the cycle, making it harder to recharge, reset, and focus on solutions.

Draw the Line Before They Cross It for You

In today's workplace, oversharing isn't just risky, it's reputational sabotage. People don't need every detail of your personal life to form an opinion about your professionalism. In fact, the more emotional baggage you bring into the office, the more likely it is to be weaponized against you.

If you turn the breakroom into your therapy room, someone else will turn your vulnerability into their advantage, and they won't have your best interest in mind.

What Not to Share at Work: The Overshare Survival Guide

The breakroom isn't a therapy room. Oversharing is career sabotage disguised as small talk. This worksheet will help you figure out what "not" to spill, spot the emotional leaks that are hurting your credibility, and draw the line before someone else turns your vulnerability into breakroom entertainment.

Part 1: Red Flag Radar
Check yourself: have you dropped any of these at work lately?

Topic	Shared Recently (☐/✘)	Why It Screams "Danger"
Relationship Drama		Instant gossip fuel. Congrats, you just became today's story.
Mental Health Diagnosis* (anxiety, depression)		Instead of compassion, some will quietly question your "stability."
Family Issues		Shifts focus from your competence to your chaos.
Financial Struggles		Signals unreliability, even if that's not true.
Conflicts with co-workers or leadership		Office politics jackpot. You just armed your rivals.
Medical Issues*		Becomes speculation or pity in disguise.
Party Behavior		People don't forget the "one time at karaoke" story.
Politics or Rants		Half the office instantly tuned out. The other half just labeled you.
Dating Apps / Hookups		Congratulations, your credibility just swiped left.

*This is not about your legal rights; it's about your reputation. HR protects laws; co-workers protect gossip.

Part 2: Reputation Reality Check
Answer honestly because denial is how people end up blindsided at review time.

1. Who at work (or in your internship, volunteer role, or even school setting) knows the most about your personal life?

2. Have they ever repeated something you said to someone else? → ☐ Yes ☐ No ☐ Not Sure

3. If your boss overheard your latest personal rant, would it help or hurt your image?

4. Do people respect you more, or pity you more, after emotional conversations?

5. Bonus gut-punch: If your most personal story were repeated in a team meeting, what headline would it create about you?

Part 3: Your New Policy
Write down 1–2 go-to phrases to shut down oversharing before it hurts you:

Examples:

- "I'm still processing some personal stuff, but let's talk shop for now."
- "That's a long story I'd rather not unpack here—how's that new client project?"

Your Version:

→ _____

→ _____

Save the therapy for your therapist. Save the venting for your group chat. At work, less drama = more credibility. The fewer distractions people tie to your name, the louder your results will speak.

THE NEGATIVITY TRAIN

The breakroom felt safe: four women leaning against the counter, swapping frustrations about their workload and poking fun at a manager's quirks. It felt like solidarity, the kind of venting that bonded people together. But behind the smiles, two of those women were already taking mental notes. By the end of the week, one of the women in that circle opened her peer evaluation and found a word she never expected: *"harmful."* The very co-workers who had laughed and vented alongside her had flipped the script, framing her as the negative one to protect their own image. What started as "just venting" had quietly become evidence against her. That's how gossip works: it feels safe in the moment, then gets weaponized when it's convenient.

Why This Matters:

Gossip feels like connection, until it derails your reputation. You don't need to take part in the negativity to feel included. Stay clear. Stay focused.

Gossip Will Derail Your Career - Fast

Once you start getting comfortable in your new job and you've made it through the awkward introductions, figured out the office coffee maker, and found your rhythm, it's easy to let your guard down. But that comfort can be a trap. Just when things feel steady, the gossip begins to feel… harmless. The office side-eyes become inside jokes. The snarky comments feel like bonding. And before you know it, you've boarded the negativity train and it's halfway out of the station before you even realize what kind of ride you're on.

Let me be clear: that train leads straight to career derailment.

I've counseled many young professionals, tearfully sitting in my office, wondering how they went from feeling included and confident to being iced out and undermined. The answer was always the same: they got too comfortable in the wrong conversations.

It starts innocently enough, venting about a project, laughing at a manager's quirks, joining in on whispered critiques about a co-worker's presentation. Those same women who "welcomed" you into the fold? They're often the first to flip the script and throw you under the bus when the moment suits them. Office politics is a game with no rules and no winners, only consequences.

Let's explore how to spot these dynamics, resist the urge to take part, and build credibility that doesn't depend on being part of the inner gossip circle.

Quick Detour: The Drama Triangle

Think gossip is the only train running through the office? Nope, there's a whole line called "The Drama Triangle" - a psychological model by Stephen Karpman that explains why workplace conflict feels like reruns. Once you know it, you'll start spotting it everywhere: in meetings, on Teams chats, even in the awkward silence around the copier.

Meet the Cast: The Three Roles
- Victim → "Why does this always happen to me?" Helpless, stuck, always sighing.
- Persecutor → "You messed this up." Critical, blaming all control—no collaboration.
- Rescuer → "Don't worry, I'll handle it." Sounds noble but ends in burnout and resentment.

These roles feed off each other: victims get sympathy, persecutors get control, rescuers get validation. But no one gets growth.

An HR Story You Won't Find in Training Videos

I once mediated a team that could've won a Tony for workplace drama. One employee always claimed to be "too busy" (victim). The manager swooped in to fix everything (rescuer). Meanwhile, another colleague got painted as the weak link (persecutor). Week after week, it was the same show: lots of emotion, zero resolution.

The fix wasn't easy, but it was simple:
- The victim had to set priorities and stop dumping.
- The rescuer had to back off and let others struggle a little.
- The persecutor had to learn direct, respectful communication.

Slowly, the cycle cracked, the triangle lost its grip, and the team finally started focusing on the work instead of the drama.

Once you know the Drama Triangle, you can't unsee it and that's your advantage. You don't have to play the victim, the villain, or the overworked hero. You can choose a new role, one that builds instead of breaks. So, the next time workplace drama starts pulling you in, ask: "What role am I playing, and how can I rewrite the script?"

Drama doesn't fuel careers, clarity does. When you step out of the triangle, you stop acting in someone else's soap opera and start directing your own story.

While not every office spat turns into a full-blown triangle, the warning signs of gossip and negativity usually show up first, like flashing red lights telling you it's time to step back before you're pulled in.

Red Flags: When the Gossip Train Is Pulling into Your Station

You won't always realize you're being pulled into office politics until it's too late. But the signs are there if you know what to look for. Here are the red flags that signal it's time to step back, smile politely, and not engage:

- **The "Safe Space" Setup:**
  When someone starts a conversation with, "Can I tell you something, just between us?" That's your cue to listen, but not agree, respond, or contribute. If they're willing to talk to you about someone, they'll eventually talk to someone about you.

- **Disguised Complaints as Camaraderie**
  "We're all thinking it, I'm just saying it out loud." This is how negativity gets normalized. It's not a bold truth-teller, it's a subtle recruiter for the petty squad. Don't take the bait.

- **The "Us vs. Them" Language**
  "Management doesn't get it." "She's always been like that." This type of talk positions you in opposition to others. It plants seeds of resentment, and the more you feed them, the harder they are to uproot.

- **Compliments with a Hidden Blade**
  "You're way better than her." That might sound flattering, but it's often said to isolate you. The goal? Get you to lower your guard, share your frustrations, and hand over ammunition that can be used against you later.

- **Sudden Silence When You Walk In**
  If the room goes quiet the second you enter, chances are… you've been the topic. And if those same people are still smiling in your face, it's time to protect your energy and your reputation.

Strategies to Rise Above Gossip

You don't have to become cold or distant to avoid workplace drama, but you do have to be intentional about how you engage. Here's how to rise above gossip without isolating yourself or losing your authenticity:

1. **Redirect with Grace**

If someone starts to gossip around you, steer the conversation without being confrontational.

Instead of: "I don't want to talk about this." Try:
- "You know, I haven't worked closely with her, I can't really say."
- "I haven't had that experience. Hopefully, it was just a bad day."

This keeps you neutral without sounding judgmental or naive.

2. **Set a Personal Boundary Phrase**

   Come up with one go-to sentence you can use when conversations start heading toward the negative. Examples:
   - "Let's not spiral, it's been a long day."
   - "I'm trying not to get caught up in any of the politics right now."
   - "I'm focusing on keeping things positive, I've got enough chaos in my inbox."

3. **Journal, Don't Vent**

   When something irritates you at work, your first instinct might be to find someone to talk to. But oversharing with a co-worker can get messy fast. Instead? Put it in a journal. Draft an email and never send it. Get the emotion out privately, then decide if it's worth acting on.

4. **Plug in with Purpose.**

   If your workspace allows, headphones can be a great tool for staying in your zone. Music, a podcast, or even white noise sends a subtle signal: "I'm focused." Fewer interruptions = fewer invitations to gossip.

5. **Be Known for Positivity, Not Participation**

   When your name comes up in conversation, let it be associated with:
   - Problem-solving
   - Getting work done
   - Having integrity
   - Staying out of drama

   The longer you support that reputation, the harder it becomes for people to paint you as part of the problem.

What If You've Already Boarded the Gossip Train?

So... you slipped. You took part in the chatter, or you even started it. Don't panic. You're not doomed, but you do need to course-correct, fast. Here's how to rebuild your reputation if you've found yourself tangled in office gossip or politics:

- ☐ **Acknowledge It to Yourself, Without Shame**

   Everyone makes mistakes. What matters more than what you did is what you do next. You don't need to make a dramatic apology to the whole team, but you do need to own it privately and commit to shifting course.

   Self-reflection: "Why did I participate? Was it boredom? Insecurity? Wanting to fit in?" Knowing your trigger helps you prevent future slips.

- ☐ **Quietly Pivot Your Behavior**

   You don't need to announce you're changing, just start living it:
   - Stop entertaining negative conversations.

- Walk away when the gossip starts.
- Refocus your conversations on work, solutions, or neutral topics.
- Build new alliances based on results, not rumors.

Over time, people will notice. Trust gets rebuilt by consistent behavior, not grand gestures.

☐ **Let Your Work Speak Louder Than Your Words**

You may not be able to undo every rumor or erase every side-eye, but you can bury it with competence:
- Show up early.
- Deliver quality work.
- Keep commitments.
- Stay solution-oriented in meetings.

Reputations are rebuilt through performance, not explanations.

☐ **Avoid Defensiveness or Playing the Victim**

If someone calls you out, don't get combative. Acknowledge. Shift. Move forward. "You're right. I got caught up in something I shouldn't have. I'm focused on moving forward." That one line says: maturity, self-awareness, growth.

☐ **Rebuild Your Inner Circle Intentionally**

Take inventory. Who benefits from your success, and who feeds off your failure? Gradually limit time with the drama dealers. Build relationships with colleagues who uplift, challenge, and support you professionally.

Know When to Pull the Emergency Brake

Every workplace has drama. The difference between sinking and succeeding isn't about avoiding it entirely, it's about knowing when to step back, shut it down, and rise above. You are not bound to ride the gossip train just because someone saved you a seat. You don't owe anyone your silence when something feels off, and you certainly don't have to let others' harmful behavior drag you off track.

Reputations are fragile. In the professional world, they travel faster than the truth. You will work too hard, and have too much potential, to let whispers and side-eyes dictate your trajectory. If you slip? Learn. Recalibrate. Move forward stronger.

The most respected women in the room aren't the ones sharing the most gossip, they're the ones too focused on building something meaningful to waste time "stirring the pot."

Negativity Train & Drama Triangle Reflection Worksheet
Don't Just Ride the Drama - Rewrite the Script

This worksheet combines two realities: gossip (the Negativity Train) and dysfunctional conflict (the Drama Triangle). Both are career derailers, and both need the same thing: awareness + action. Use this page to spot the traps, name your patterns, and practice better exits.

Part 1: Spotting Your Stops on the Negativity Train

Think back to the last time you felt pulled into gossip or unwanted drama. Check what applies:
☐ I joined in because I didn't want to feel left out.
☐ I stayed quiet, but my silence made it look like I agreed.
☐ I added my own complaint to "bond."
☐ I laughed along, even though it made me uncomfortable.
☐ I tried to fix it but ended up stuck in the drama anyway.

What triggered you to get pulled in?
_____

What was the impact on your reputation (real or perceived)?
_____

Part 2: Identify Your Drama Triangle Role(s)
When tension hits, which role do you slip into most often?
☐ Victim → "Why does this always happen to me?"
☐ Persecutor → "This is YOUR fault."
☐ Rescuer → "Don't worry, I'll fix it."
☐ Bystander → "If I ignore this, maybe it'll go away."

Under stress, my default role is:
_____

Why do I think I fall into this role?
_____

Part 3: Situational Awareness
Think of a recent messy situation (gossip, conflict, or side-eyes at the breakroom table).

What happened?
___

Which role did you play?
___

Which role(s) did others play?
___

What was the outcome? Did anything get solved, or just recycled?
___

Part 4: Rewrite the Scene

Flip the script:
If you were the Victim, how could you have shifted to Creator (taking ownership, not pity)?
___

If you were the Persecutor, how could you have shifted to Challenger (offering growth, not blame)?
___

If you were the Rescuer, how could you have shifted to Coach (supporting without saving)?
___

If gossip were the trigger, what boundary phrase could you have used to redirect the conversation?
___

Part 5: Your Personal Exit Strategy

What's one specific move you'll make the next time gossip or drama shows up?
(Examples: "I'll walk away," "I'll redirect the convo," "I'll keep my notes to myself instead of venting.")
___

Final Reflection

One action I will take this week to avoid boarding the Negativity Train or stepping into the Drama Triangle is:
___

Remember: Every time you refuse to gossip or shift out of Victim/Persecutor/Rescuer mode, you're not just protecting your reputation, you're rewriting the culture in the room.

EMOTIONAL LABOR 101

I once watched a young professional spend more time smoothing over her manager's moods than doing her actual job. Every morning, she gauged the temperature of the office: Was her boss slamming drawers? Silent? Chatty? Before she opened a single email, she adjusted her tone, her energy, and even her facial expressions just to keep the peace. Her performance review praised her "team player" attitude. But not once did it recognize the invisible work - the unpaid, unacknowledged job of managing emotions - that left her drained before lunch.

The Unseen Job Description

This is emotional labor: the effort of regulating, monitoring, and absorbing other people's emotions so the workplace doesn't implode. It's not in the handbook, but it's everywhere. Answering emails with extra exclamation points so a co-worker won't read your message as cold. Laughing at a manager's bad jokes to protect their ego. Sitting through another story about a colleague's weekend even though your own deadlines are drowning you. It's the quiet expectation that women will be the emotional glue holding teams together.

Why It Falls on Women

Emotional labor is not evenly distributed. Women, especially young professionals, often inherit it by default. Generations before us were told to "keep everyone happy," and that legacy lingers. Women are praised for being approachable, nurturing, and collaborative, but punished if they push back, disengage, or stop catering to others' moods. Meanwhile, men who skip emotional labor rarely face consequences, because the system doesn't expect it of them.

When Women Enforce It on Other Women

Here's the part we don't always talk about: women are often the ones demanding this labor from each other. A senior woman might say to a younger colleague, "Don't rock the boat, just keep things smooth." Another might roll her eyes if a peer doesn't smile enough in meetings or doesn't volunteer to plan the baby shower. In the worst cases, women use emotional labor as a control tactic: assigning it, withholding recognition for it, or punishing those who won't perform it.

Sometimes it's subtle. A female manager might expect her female staff to handle the "soft stuff" - consoling the upset employee, organizing the team lunch, cleaning up after a meeting - while excusing male colleagues from the same tasks. Other times, it's blunt: "You need to lighten up, or people won't like working with you." The message is clear: your career isn't just about results - it's about how well you can absorb, manage, and smooth over everyone else's feelings.

The Double Bind

This creates a vicious cycle. Women who refuse emotional labor risk being labeled cold, unlikable, or "not a team player." Women who absorb it all become exhausted and resentful. And women who enforce it on others reinforce the very dynamics that keep all of us stuck. The result? Emotional labor becomes both a weapon and a leash.

Once You Take It On, It Sticks

Once you become the go-to person for emotional labor, it's hard to shake. People remember the person who planned the last birthday lunch, calmed down the angry client, or diffused tension after a heated meeting. You become the unofficial "fixer." And in many workplaces, once you've proven you'll do it, it silently becomes part of your job description.

The danger is that being the fixer can hold you back. Leaders may see you as *too valuable in that role* to move up. Why promote the person who smooths over every meltdown when the team "needs" her right where she is? Advancement opportunities slip by, not because you lack talent, but because your invisible labor has become your identity. You're not seen as the strategist, the innovator, or the leader - you're seen as the emotional safety net.

Take Shannon, for example. She was the employee everyone turned to when a project derailed or when two personalities clashed. She was praised constantly as "the glue that holds the team together." But when a leadership position opened, she was passed over. The reason? Her boss said, "We just can't afford to lose you in your current role because you keep the team stable." In other words, her talent for fixing problems became the very reason she wasn't allowed to advance beyond them.

The problem? Unlike a real job duty, you won't get recognition, pay, or promotion credit for it, only more of the same. What was once a "thank you" quickly turns into "we'll just let her handle it," locking you in place while others move forward.

💬 *If you're always the fixer, you risk becoming indispensable but invisible.*

Signs of Emotional Labor Burnout

Like any other form of overwork, emotional labor has a breaking point. The difference is that burnout here doesn't come from late nights with spreadsheets, it comes from constantly carrying everyone else's emotions. Signs include:
- Chronic exhaustion that doesn't match your actual workload.
- Irritability or resentment toward co-workers you're "taking care of."
- Feeling invisible - like your real work doesn't matter compared to your soothing role.
- Loss of empathy - when you've given so much you have nothing left for yourself.
- Anxiety before interactions, because you know you'll have to manage not just the conversation but the emotions swirling around it.

If you ever experience these symptoms, it may not be the job tasks burning you out - it may be the unpaid, unspoken job of emotional labor draining you dry.

Breaking the Cycle

The first step is recognizing emotional labor for what it is: real work, even if it's invisible. Once you name it, you can begin to loosen its grip. But breaking the cycle requires both personal boundaries *and* cultural shifts among women.

1. Set Clear Boundaries Without Apology

You don't need to explain away every "no." Practice simple, direct language that sets limits while remaining professional:
- "I'm focused on this deadline and can't take on the event planning right now."
- "That sounds important. Let's make sure it's assigned fairly so it doesn't always land on the same people."
- "I want to stay focused on my role—I'm not the best person to mediate this."

Boundaries don't make you difficult; they make you sustainable.

2. Redistribute the Load

Emotional labor is often invisible until someone points it out. Instead of absorbing it, put it on the table for discussion:
- Suggest a rotating system for office "extras" like celebrations, organizing lunches, or onboarding new hires.
- Ask in meetings: *"Who's capturing action items?"* instead of letting it silently default to the same woman.
- Encourage leaders to recognize emotional work in performance reviews - or better yet, to stop assuming it belongs only to women.

3. Stop Handing It Down to Other Women

Here's where women oppress women: by expecting younger or junior women to take on what we're tired of doing. "Let the intern plan it." "She's new - she can stay late with him." These micro-assignments perpetuate the very cycle we say we hate. Breaking it means refusing to pass the torch of unpaid emotional cleanup to the next woman in line.

4. Redefine What Leadership Looks Like

Too often, emotional labor is framed as "leadership potential," when in reality it's unpaid maintenance. True leadership isn't smoothing over every outburst; it's setting norms, so outbursts don't derail the work in the first place. Push back on the idea that being the office peacekeeper equals readiness for promotion. Leadership is strategy, influence, and decision-making - not babysitting egos.

5. Build Alliances, Not Just Resistance

One of the strongest ways to break the cycle is collective visibility. If you see another woman constantly saddled with emotional labor, name it. Back her up when she sets a boundary. Normalize phrases like:
- "We've asked her to handle this a lot. Let's rotate."
- "She's done the last three of these - it's someone else's turn."

Alone, pushing back can feel risky. Together, it becomes culture change.

6. Redefine Empathy as a Shared Skill

The goal isn't to strip empathy out of the workplace. The goal is to make it everyone's responsibility, not an unpaid second job for women. When empathy and relational skills are expected from all genders, emotional labor stops being invisible "women's work" and starts being part of a balanced culture.

Here's Why This Matters

Breaking the cycle of emotional labor doesn't mean abandoning compassion - it means refusing to let compassion be weaponized as a career limiter. If we keep carrying it alone, we'll keep being indispensable but invisible. But if we set boundaries, stop passing it down, and demand shared responsibility, emotional labor transforms from an invisible trap into a visible, manageable piece of workplace culture.

Reflection & Reset: Emotional Labor 101

Part 1: Picture It
Imagine you're starting your first job. A few weeks in, your manager asks you to "just take notes" during every meeting. At the same time, a teammate vents to you daily about her frustrations, and your boss praises you for being "so easy to talk to."

Write down: How would you feel if this became your routine?

Part 2: Spot the Hidden Pattern
Emotional labor is sneaky because it often hides inside "being nice" or "being a team player."
- Think about school, sports, or volunteer groups you've been part of. Were you ever expected to smooth things over, organize extras, or take care of everyone else's feelings?

Write one example here:

Part 3: Future Red Flags
Circle any situations that might signal emotional labor in your first job:
- Being asked to plan social events because "you're good at it."
- Feeling pressure to smile or laugh when you don't want to.
- Being the one people vent to about problems you can't fix.
- Doing tasks outside your role to keep peace in the team.
- Being praised for "holding everyone together" but not for your actual work.

Which of these would bother you the most, and why?

Part 4: Write Your Boundary Scripts
Practice now so it's easier later. Fill in the blanks:
- "I appreciate being asked, but I want to stay focused on _____."
- "I think it's important that _____ also gets a chance to do this."
- "I understand this is frustrating. Let's bring it up with _____ instead of me."

Which script feels the most natural for you to use? Circle it.

Part 5: Promise Yourself

One day, you'll be in a position of influence. When that happens, don't hand emotional labor down to the next woman.

Complete this sentence:

When I have authority, I will not expect _____ just because she's a woman.

Takeaway: Emotional labor doesn't have to be your invisible job. The earlier you can spot it, the easier it will be to set boundaries and build a career based on your skills, not your ability to keep everyone else comfortable.

BOSS ≠ FRIEND

It's tempting, especially when you're new, eager, and trying to make a good impression, to blur the line between boss and friend. After all, your boss laughs at your jokes, tosses emojis in Teams, and insists "we're all a family here." But don't get it twisted; the same person smiling with you today could be the one critiquing you in tomorrow's performance review. That's because your boss is not your friend. They may be approachable, even fun, but they sign your paycheck, not your yearbook. Their role is to evaluate you, decide your raise, and, if necessary, make the hard call to let you go. That doesn't make them the villain, it just makes them the boss. This isn't high school, and you're not campaigning for prom queen.

Why It Matters

When boundaries are blurred, communication gets messy. A boss-friend might avoid giving you the tough feedback you need to grow, or worse, they might manipulate your loyalty when things go sideways.

I once watched a young employee cry in a bathroom stall because the same boss who joined her on margarita Mondays laid her off without warning. Why? "It wasn't personal. It was just business."

Real Talk: Boundaries You Can't Skip

If you blur the lines with your boss, you're the one who pays the price. Protect yourself by drawing these boundaries early, before things get messy. DON'T:

- Vent to your boss about your co-workers, roommate drama, or ex who just slid into your DMs.
- Overshare medical issues or financial struggles with bosses; personal info isn't just gossiping fuel, it's leverage.

- Assume they'll advocate for you when push comes to shove. Their loyalty lies with the company.
- Go out for drinks and spill tea. What feels like bonding today can end up in your personnel file tomorrow.
- Friend your boss on social media. Your memes, hot takes, and beach selfies do not need to be part of your annual review vibe.

The Downside of Boss-Friendships

What seems like a bond can quickly become a blind spot. When you confuse friendliness for real friendship, you might:

- Misread their behavior and expect favors they're not able to give.
- Ignore red flags, assuming they have your best interest at heart.
- Get caught in the middle of organizational politics without realizing it.

One woman I worked with got so close to her boss that they texted daily, lunched weekly, and even went on family camping trips together. But when layoffs came, her role was eliminated. Her boss? Silent. She admitted later, "I couldn't risk anyone thinking I showed favoritism." She lost her job and the illusion of friendship in the same 15-minute meeting.

Another HR gem: a new hire friended her boss on Instagram and tagged them in "Sunday Funday" brunch selfies. When she later requested PTO for exhaustion, the boss pulled up her posts: "If you're so tired, why were you at bottomless mimosas last weekend?" Yikes.

When Friendship Ends But the Job Doesn't

What happens if the "friendship" goes sideways. You disagreed and the boss didn't like your pushback and the vibe just shifted. Here's the problem: you are still working there. That's when closeness turns into collateral. Everything you once shared - your stress, your struggles, your late-night texts - can now color their perception of you. Suddenly, credibility is questioned, and professionalism is scrutinized. Not fair - but predictable.

What If They Try to Be Friends?

Sometimes it's not you pushing for closeness, it's them. Your boss invites you to happy hours, texts outside of work, or vents about their problems. It feels flattering, even exciting, but it's also a trap if you're not careful.

How to Stay Professional Without Being a Buzzkill:

- Keep conversations centered on work. *"I'd love to circle back to that project update, want to schedule something next week?"*
- When invited to drinks after hours, politely decline. *"Thanks for the invite! I've got a standing commitment, but I'll catch you tomorrow."*

- Don't reciprocate oversharing. Neutral works: *"That sounds tough, I hope things settle down."*
- Use humor to redirect. *"I'm trying to keep my inbox under control and my personal life under wraps, it's a full-time job!"*

You don't have to be rude or cold; you just must be clear.

What Your Boss Is Actually Thinking

Most bosses want their teams to like them. But behind the scenes, they're still measuring your:

- Dependability
- Output
- Attitude
- Alignment with company culture

You may think your weekend hiking stories bring you closer. They might think: *"Great, another boundary I'll need to manage."* Remember, a boss's primary duty is to the company, not to your social calendar. The friendlier you are, the more awkward it gets when accountability is needed.

Reality Check

You can, and should, have a friendly relationship with your boss. But don't confuse friendliness with friendship. One is professional warmth. The other? Potential career chaos. Your boss doesn't need to be your friend. They need to know you can deliver - that's it.

You can be respected, trusted, and appreciated, without being emotionally entangled. That's how careers grow and how you stay ready for your next move, without feeling betrayed if things shift.

PROFESSIONAL ETIQUETTE

You might've aced your exams, polished your resume, and nailed the interview, but there's a whole hidden curriculum you weren't graded on: professional etiquette.

If you take away *nothing else* from this book, let it be this: mastering professional etiquette is one of the biggest career boosters you'll ever have. These small, often overlooked behaviors can open doors, earn respect, and keep your reputation rock solid even when your skills are still catching up. Professional etiquette doesn't cost a thing, but it pays like equity.

Professional etiquette isn't about being old-fashioned or stiff. It's about respect for the work, the people doing it, and for yourself. It's the invisible framework that shapes how others perceive your competence, reliability, and emotional intelligence. These are the basic, foundational behaviors that show others: *I'm here to be taken seriously.*

What You Signal Without Saying a Word

Let's talk about those "small" things that send huge messages:

- Looking at your phone during a meeting says, "I don't value your time."
- Typing away on your laptop while someone is presenting says, "Whatever you're saying isn't worth my full attention."
- Walking in late to meetings, events, or appointments says, "My time matters more than yours."
- Whispering or side-chatting during someone else's presentation says, "This isn't important to me."

Even if you see senior co-workers doing it, don't follow their lead! That's not a green light. That's their passive-aggressive way of undermining someone, and it reflects poorly on them.

Real talk from the HR chair: I've seen high-potential women lose credibility fast, not because of their work, but because they interrupted senior leaders, showed up unprepared, and fired off emoji-filled follow-up emails. Their talent got overshadowed by small, but costly etiquette missteps.

Professional etiquette is how you express your personal brand without saying a word. It communicates whether you're someone who can be trusted, someone who listens, and someone who shows up fully. Those "silent signals" are constantly being read by people around you: peers, supervisors, clients, and executives alike.

Show Up - Literally and Figuratively

Etiquette isn't about how you act once you're in the room, it starts with how you show up in the first place. The simplest habits set the tone for how seriously people take you. Miss these basics, and you've already lost ground before anyone even hears you speak.

1. **Always be on time**. If you're working in an appointment-based field - healthcare, finance, consulting - being late isn't just rude, it's disruptive. You're not just delaying your meeting; you're throwing off someone else's entire day. If you're running late, communicate - a quick message or call that says, "I'm running behind by 10 minutes, my apologies," goes a long way.

2. **Don't ghost your commitments.** If you say you're going to do it, then do it, and do it on time. Nothing erodes trust faster than flaking on a deadline, skipping a meeting, or forgetting a follow-through. Reliability is currency in the workplace. Every time you deliver when you said you would, you're cashing in on credibility. Every time you don't, you give someone else a reason to question your professionalism.

3. **Show up prepared**. Walking into a meeting clueless is like showing up to a test without studying everyone notices, and no one forgets. Read the agenda. Skim the background docs. Know who's in the room and what matters to them. Preparation isn't about looking competent, it's about armor, because other women are watching. If you drop the ball, it won't just be a mistake, it'll be gossiping fuel. Being prepared cuts off their chance to label you as "sloppy" or "dead weight." Instead of handing them ammunition, it hands you credibility.

4. **Respect starts with names.** Get them right: pronounce and spell them correctly. If you don't know - ask. Nothing says "I don't value you" faster than butchering someone's name out of laziness.

5. **Respond to emails like they matter.** Every message you send is a receipt of your professionalism. Do not use emojis in work responses unless the culture openly calls for it (and even then, use sparingly). Start with a greeting, end with a sign-off, and for the love of your career, use punctuation and complete sentences. Sloppy, rushed emails don't just make you look careless, but they

make you look unprofessional. Clear, polished responses show respect, competence, and maturity. Remember: emails live forever. Write like they'll be sent to your boss, or your boss's boss.

6. **Think before you speak.** Don't blurt out every idea or correction that comes to mind. If your first instinct is to prove you're smart, pause. You don't want to come across as a know-it-all, especially early on. Instead, ask yourself: *Does this add value? Am I offering insight, or just trying to impress?*

Practicing professional etiquette is one of the most underrated yet powerful tools in your career toolbox. It's more than simply good manners, it's how you build credibility, earn respect, and open doors.

Etiquette levels the playing field. It doesn't require a degree, a fancy title, or years of experience. Anyone can practice it, and everyone benefits from it. When you treat people with consistent respect, regardless of their job title or how they treat you, you're communicating something powerful: *I understand the assignment. I know how to work in a professional environment.*

Etiquette Doesn't Just Elevate You - It Protects You.

When people recall interactions, they often remember how you made them feel more than what you said. Were you courteous? Respectful? Considerate? Those impressions last. In workplaces where bias can creep into decisions, professionalism becomes your shield.

It also helps you navigate tricky situations with grace. When you act with etiquette, even when others don't, you defuse drama, deescalate conflict, and keep your integrity. It's your personal insurance policy against being labeled "difficult," "immature," or "unprofessional."

Here's the bonus: people talk. They'll mention you in rooms you're not in. How you treat others, especially those with no power over you, will echo. Professional etiquette shows emotional intelligence, maturity, and self-respect. It's a quiet power and when done right, it sets you apart in a sea of noise.

So, while others are busy trying to stand out with noise, be the one who stands out with respect. That's the kind of professionalism people remember and promote.

LOST SKILLS THAT STILL MATTER

Some of the most career-defining skills aren't taught in school, listed on a syllabus, or included in onboarding. They're the small, everyday competencies that signal professionalism and they absolutely shape how seriously you're taken. Especially if you're young and new, these "little" things can build your credibility or quietly erode it.

Older women in the workplace will notice these habits, even if they never say a word. Ignore them, and you risk being underestimated. Master them, and you stand out.

The Cursive Test

Can you read a handwritten note? Can you write one? Many Boomers and Gen X colleagues still use cursive, for feedback, thank-you cards, or quick notes left on your desk. If you treat it like ancient hieroglyphics, you'll look unprepared.

Why it matters: You don't need to use cursive daily, but being able to read it avoids embarrassment and shows respect across generations.

Envelopes Still Exist

Yes, even today. Whether mailing paperwork, sending a condolence card, or returning official documents, you should know how to address an envelope.

Basics:
- Return address on the top left.
- Full name and title of the recipient.
- Clear, neat handwriting.

Why it matters: Digital is default, but analog professionalism still stands out. Doing it correctly signals polish and maturity.

Writing a Professional Letter

This isn't about long reports or academic writing; it's about professional letters.

What matters is tone, format, and clarity. Whether it's a cover letter, a thank-you note, or a letter of concern, the goal is to be concise, respectful, and polished.

- Use a formal greeting ("Dear Ms. Parker," not "Hey").
- Stay focused and to the point.
- Proofread. Twice.
- End with a professional sign-off ("Sincerely," "Best regards").

Why it matters: Professional writing shows emotional intelligence and respect for context. It communicates maturity without you saying a word.

Email ≠ Texting.

Emails are not DMs. Professionalism lives in the details: punctuation, spelling, and tone. Every emoji, exclamation point, and ellipsis sends a message.

Avoid:
- "Hey!!" as a greeting
- No subject line
- All lowercase.
- Text-speak (LOL, OMG)

Do:
- Use a clear subject line.
- Greet the recipient by name.
- Keep tone polite and professional—even when frustrated.

Why it matters: Poorly written emails get forwarded, screen-grabbed, and remembered. Don't let sloppy communication define your brand.

Voicemail Isn't Dead

Some industries still rely on it - especially HR, healthcare, law, and finance. A confident voicemail sets you apart.

Formula:
1. Say your full name slowly.
2. State the reason for your call.
3. Leave your number twice (beginning and end).
4. Keep it under 30 seconds.

Why it matters: A clear voicemail signals preparation, confidence, and respect for someone's time.

Don't "Reply All" Unless You Mean To

Always double-check your recipients before hitting send.

Why it matters: Accidentally cluttering inboxes with unnecessary responses screams newcomer mistakes. It's the digital version of shouting in a quiet room.

Handwritten Notes Still Win

You don't need fancy stationery. Just a card and a pen. A thank-you after an interview, a congratulations card, or a thoughtful "thinking of you" goes a long way.

Why it matters: Effort stands out. Handwritten notes say, "*I value you enough to take the time.*"

Basic Tech Tasks You Should Master

No one expects you to be IT, but fumbling through the basics makes you look unprepared. You should be able to:

- Convert files to PDF.
- Zip/unzip folders.
- Use Track Changes in Word.
- Format a PowerPoint cleanly.
- Schedule a Zoom with a password.
- Share a file link (not the file itself).
- Upload with correct naming conventions.

*Why it matters***:** Small tech skills save everyone time and prevent you from being "the person someone else has to fix."

Actually Learn Microsoft Office

Corporate, government, nonprofit, and healthcare organizations still run on Microsoft Word, Excel, PowerPoint, and Outlook. Being "bad at Excel" isn't quirky - it's a red flag.

Excel essentials:
- SUM, AVERAGE, IF formulas.
- Sorting/filtering data.
- Freezing header rows.
- Creating and formatting tables.
- Conditional formatting.
- Pivot tables (basic familiarity is enough).

Other musts:
- Track changes in Word.
- Build clean, professional decks in PowerPoint.
- Schedule meetings in Outlook (time zones included).
- Use OneDrive or SharePoint links properly.

Why it matters: Competence with Microsoft Office is the language of professional credibility. Walk in fluent, and you build trust fast.

Your Workspace Talks - What's It Saying?

Your desk is an extension of your professional presence.

Don't:
- Overload with personal photos or vacation snapshots.
- Overdecorate with glitter signs or neon clutter in conservative

environments.
- Leave personal care items (lotions, nail files, perfumes) in plain sight.

Do:
- Add one or two tasteful items, like a framed photo or small plant.
- Use clean, neutral accessories.
- Keep it tidy—clutter signals distraction.

Why it matters: Your workspace speaks before you do. Keep it professional and aligned with your environment.

Final Thought: Don't Hand Them Ammunition

You may think some of these skills are outdated. You may even have faster, sharper ways of working. But here's the reality: many workplaces are still led by Boomers and Gen Xers; leaders who built careers by mastering these fundamentals. To them, these aren't quirks, they're standards.

Don't give them reasons to doubt your professionalism. These basics aren't about playing small; they're about playing smart. When you master the hidden curriculum, you're not just surviving, you're standing out.

Learn etiquette. Master the tools. Adapt to the environment. And when you're surrounded by women who are quick to judge? You'll have the credibility and composure to shut down their doubts before they ever find a crack to exploit.

THE ENDING IS THE BEGINNING

If you've made it this far, you've already chosen courage over comfort. You're willing to face what many avoid: that sometimes the sharpest cuts at work don't always come from men, but from other women. When women cling to power as if there's only one seat at the table, the culture suffers. By confronting this truth, you're already starting to change it.

The next step is understanding what that truth means for you. Once you see these dynamics clearly, you can stop taking them personally. A snide remark isn't always about your ability - it's about someone else's insecurity. A closed door doesn't mean you don't belong - it means the person guarding it is afraid of losing control. When you separate who you are from the behavior aimed at you, you strip that behavior of its power.

That awareness is your advantage. Where others step into their careers unaware, you carry a light in the dark. You notice the dismissive glances, the cliques, and the "jokes" that land like daggers. Now, instead of being blindsided, you're prepared. You're no longer here to play naïve - you're here to play aware.

When you begin to rewrite the code, you don't just change how you work, you disrupt patterns that have gone unquestioned for decades. You will stumble, you'll take hits, and you will still meet women who doubt you, dismiss you, or quietly undermine you to protect their own standing. There will be moments when your voice shakes, when your confidence wavers, and when the weight of competing expectations feels heavier than your job description. But those moments don't define you, they shape you. They are not signs that you don't belong; they are proof that you are navigating the same unspoken terrain generations of women before you stumbled through. The difference is that now you see it for what it is.

This book began with my own confusion: how could all the slogans, seminars, and leadership retreats promise empowerment yet never name the harder truth: that too often, oppression in the workplace comes dressed in lipstick and heels? We've all been told to "work hard and be nice," but no one prepares you for the gossip, the exclusion, or the subtle sabotage that can quietly derail your career. This book stripped the varnish off that story. It revealed the code beneath the culture and provided you with a survival guide no one else dared to write until now.

Along the way, you were introduced to the workplace essentials:

- **Reputation is currency.** You spend it with every outfit, every email, every word you speak - or choose not to.
- **Boundaries are your shield.** From dating at work to oversharing in the breakroom, you now know that protecting your peace is not selfish; it's strategy.
- **Gossip and oversharing kill careers.** The negativity train always derails into whispers and doubt, and you've learned how to stay off it.
- **Emotional labor has limits.** Being the office "therapist" or "mom" isn't a path to leadership; it's a drain disguised as praise. You now know when to say no.
- **Professional etiquette is equity.** Names, punctuality, preparation, polished communication - these aren't fluff. They are survival skills that protect your credibility when everything else is judged more harshly.
- **And hardest of all:** the battles you face won't always come from men in power. Too often, they'll come from women who should've been allies. But now, you'll never be blindsided by it again.

Together, these lessons aren't just survival tactics - they are the building blocks of breaking the cycle and reshaping the culture for the women who come after you.

Awareness changes everything. It doesn't mean you'll avoid every wound, but it means you'll recover faster, pivot smarter, and rise stronger. You'll know which battles are worth fighting and which whispers to ignore. And every time you choose clarity over gossip, boundaries over burnout, and courage over compliance, you're not just protecting yourself, you're rewriting the code for everyone who comes after you.

That's how change begins. Not with slogans, posters, or another panel on "women's leadership," but with women deciding to do it differently. To extend a hand where none was extended to them. To say, "Let me show you," instead of "Figure it out." To stop weaponizing kindness, gossip, or silence against each other and instead model something future generations can build on.

Because the interns are watching and the new hires are listening. The next generation of women is taking mental notes, not just on what you achieve, but on how you achieve it. When they see you set boundaries, speak truth, or recover from sabotage without shrinking, you've given them something no seminar ever could: a living, breathing example of how to rise without repeating the cycle. That's the ripple effect and that's your legacy.

So, when the moment comes - and it will - when the sabotage shows up as silence, exclusion, or subtle eye rolls, you won't shrink or play along. You'll hold your ground, show up with clarity, and let your presence say what needs to be said: *"This is how we do it differently."*

Here's your choice:

Option One: Play Along.

You can mimic what's been done before you. You can hoard information, undermine the new girl, and pull the ladder up behind you. You can confuse fear for power and cruelty for respect. But let's be real - that's not strength – it's recycling harm and keeping the cycle alive.

Option Two: Rewrite the Code.

You can redefine what power looks like. It doesn't have to mean perfection, intimidation, or silence. Real strength is choosing excellence without turning everyone else into competition and sharing the credit when it's due. It's using your voice to amplify the woman who isn't in the room. It's mentoring the one who challenges you instead of shrinking back in fear, not because you're obligated to, but because you're capable of it.

This is bigger than just you and your career. It's about the culture women create for each other every single day. Do we keep repeating the same scarcity games? Or do we choose empathy over ego, collaboration over competition, connection over criticism?

This book wasn't about fixing you. You were never broken. It was about helping you see the system for what it is and giving you the awareness to survive it, outsmart it, and rewrite it.

This isn't the tidy conclusion of a book; it's the opening scene of your movement. You've been introduced to the unspoken code of sabotage, silence, and side-eyes that too often define women's workplaces, and now you hold the power to rewrite it. From this point forward, every boundary you set, every rumor you refuse to fuel, and every choice to support instead of sabotage becomes part of a new script. It won't always be easy; there will be bumps, bruises, and moments when others still try to pull you back into the old game. But you'll know better now. You'll recognize it for what it is, rise faster because of it, and carry yourself with a strength that cannot be ignored.

This ending is your beginning to break the culture code. By rewriting it, you turn a workplace that once masked oppression behind lipstick and heels into a culture where women rise together with respect, trust, and encouragement.

CULTURE CODE RECAP

When sabotage shows up in side-eyes, silence, or whispered "feedback," don't freeze. Flip back to this code and remind yourself what matters most:

The Hardest Battles Aren't Always With Men
- Some of the sharpest cuts come from women.
- Expect it. Don't be shocked by it. Don't let it define you.
- Learn to spot sabotage early and set boundaries that protect your path.

Reputation is Currency
- Every email, outfit, and comment spends or saves it.
- Perception can outweigh performance, so manage both.
- Don't give gossipers free ammo.

Boundaries Are Your Shield
- Don't date where you get your direct deposit.
- The breakroom is not a therapy room.
- Say "No" early and often, it's protection, not selfishness.

Gossip Kills Careers
- The "negativity train" feels like connection, until it derails your credibility.
- If the room goes silent when you walk in, odds are you've been the topic.

Emotional Labor Has Limits
- You're not the unpaid office therapist.
- Carrying the team's morale won't get you promoted.
- Spot burnout before it buries you: tired, resentful, invisible = red flags.

Etiquette is Equity
- Show up on time, prepared, and polished.
- Emails aren't DMs: punctuation, tone, and clarity matter.
- Respect names, respect time, respect the room. Small habits = big signals.

Your Boss Isn't Your Friend
- They sign your review, not your yearbook.
- Keep it professional: no venting, no oversharing, no Sunday Funday tags. Warmth is fine, blurred lines are not.

Want the words to back up your boundaries?

Saboteurs in heels don't stand a chance if you've got the right script. *Script for Success: Turn Tough Talks into Career Wins* is your next step. This book gave you the survival code, *Script for Success* gives you the exact language to enforce it. From shutting down gossip to holding your ground in the moments that matter, it arms you with sharp, professional scripts that turn tough talks into career wins. Boundaries protect you, but words make them unbreakable.

ABOUT THE AUTHOR

Leslie Baker has spent over twenty years in HR watching workplace politics unfold like a bad reality show, only with fewer commercial breaks and way more paperwork. She's counseled employees crying in bathroom stalls, mediated shouting matches over who "stole" the stapler and watched women sabotage each other with side-eyes sharper than any performance review. She knows the unspoken rules, the power plays, and the gossip networks that run most offices, because she's had to clean up the mess when they backfire. Out of those boardroom battles and breakroom blowups came *Hustle & Harvest Co.*, her platform to arm professionals with straight-up truths, unapologetic tools, and the scripts no leadership seminar will ever hand you. Leslie doesn't just write about culture - she's survived it, mediated it, and now she's rewriting the code so you can do more than endure it. In a world where oppression sometimes wears lipstick and heels, Leslie is here to remind you: you can wear your own and stomp past the sabotage, leaving your heel marks in victory.

Saboteurs in heels don't stand a chance if you've got the right words. Get your copy of Script for Success: Turn Tough Talks Into Career Wins! on Amazon and start talking like a pro.

www.ingramcontent.com/pod-product-compliance
Lightning Source LLC
Chambersburg PA
CBHW080947050426
42337CB00055B/4584